Felipe Santander

THREE PLAYS

A Smith and Kraus Book
Published by Smith and Kraus, Inc.
177 Lyme Road, Hanover, NH 03755
www.smithkraus.com

First Edition: April 2002
10 9 8 7 6 5 4 3 2 1

Cover and Text Design by Julia Hill Gignoux, Freedom Hill Design

The Library of Congress Cataloging-In-Publication Data

Santander, Felipe, 1934–2002
[Plays. English. Selections]
Felipe Santander : three plays / translated by Lynne Alvarez.
p. cm. — (Great translations series)
ISBN 1-57525-264-3
1. Santander, Felipe, 1934–2002—Translations into English. I. Title: Three plays.
II. Alvarez, Lynne.
III. Title. IV. Great translations for actors series.
PQ7298.29.A454 A23 2002
862'.64—dc21
2002276539

Felipe Santander

THREE PLAYS

Translated by Lynne Alvarez

Great Translations Series

SK
A Smith and Kraus Book

It is not the usual practice to dedicate a book to its translator, but then, it is unusual to have a translator like Lynne Alvarez. One good turn deserves another . . .

To Lynne Alvarez, for having read all my work, having selected and translated the three plays included in this collection, and for her talent, hard work, and generosity.

Contents

In Memorium
A Few Words from the Translator

On Tuesday, November 6, 2001 — only days before we received the final galleys for this book — Felipe Santander, one of Mexico's foremost contemporary playwrights, died in his home in the Mexican village of Ocotepec just outside of Cuernavacas. He was sixty-eight. He will be sorely missed by all of us who knew him for his delightful presence — the piquancy of his humor, the theatricality of his intelligence, and the depth of his passions. Though we are bereft of the man, he has bequeathed us a wealth of these qualities in his plays — three of which I have translated for this collection. Fortunately he was also pressed to write prefatory notes to his plays in which we can glimpse a more personal view of what I would call his "ironic realism." I believe he eludes the soubriquets of "magical realist" or "fatalist" too facilely applied to Latin American writers, for Felipe's plays tell us, "Yes, the system stinks, yes, we are flawed, yes, strange forces affect our lives, see how our attempts at individual heroism fail, but there are the reasons why. We must act together and consciously to change this misery. We must unite. Watch me, join me! Act!"

Felipe Santander was a man of his word and a man of action. He fought for his country as an agricultural engineer working among the peasants and the "ejidatarios." He fought for the arts as a playwright, a director, an actor, a composer, a producer, and a teacher. He brought Arthur Miller's work to Ocotepec and brought his created village of Tenochtlen to the Public Theater in New York City.

I fervently hope this collection of his plays in translation serves both as an introduction of his work to a wider English-speaking public and as a tribute to this most worldly and most Mexican of men.

Lynne Alvarez
Cherry Valley, New York
December 2001

Introduction

Felipe Santander loves to play with genres. In the dizzyingly diverse worlds of the three exciting works included in this volume, you'll see him take familiar styles and stand them on their heads. He reinvents the political thriller, the Kafkaesque nightmare, and the coming-of-age formats and creates wholly new uses for them. It's this bold theatricality that makes his work so universal even as the roots of his plays are buried deep in Mexican soil.

"Poor Mexico! So far from God and so close to the United States." Such were the words ascribed to General Porfirio Diaz, Mexico's "Great Dictator" and against whom the Mexican revolution was waged. Mexico's proximity to the U.S. has defined much of its modern history even as we've managed as best we could to ignore the rich culture to our south. Author Alan Riding captured this paradox in the apt title of his "portrait of the Mexicans," *Distant Neighbors*. We are indeed close *and* far from each other or, as Riding puts it, "Probably nowhere in the world do two countries as different as Mexico and the United States live side by side . . . the two countries are separated by language, religion, race, philosophy, and history. The United States is a nation barely two hundred years and is lunging for the (future). Mexico is several thousand years old and is still held back by its past."

In Santander's plays we have an easily accessible window by which to peek into that very different world. His multiple ways of telling stories are all quickly understandable and invigorating while the world he depicts is sometimes as distant to us as the dark side of the moon.

If that weren't riches enough, we also have the razor-sharp yet fluid translations of Lynne Alvarez to guide us through the terrain. It's a great boon to have such an accomplished writer as Alvarez bringing us Santander's world. She shares his passion for political dialogue sans preaching and her distinguished career as a playwright insures that she understands his structural innovations while her skills as a poet bring us Santander's Spanish in lively English.

Santander began his theatrical career as an actor and soon became something of a matinee idol in Mexico. But when he began to turn to play writing, he soon veered from the boulevard style he knew so well to plays with a political punch. That didn't endear him to the government, which worked hard to keep his plays out of the theaters (most all of which in Mexico are state-owned). But what he had to say couldn't be silenced. Thus, for example, the second play in this anthology, *The Agronomist*, went on to become the longest-running play in the history of Mexican theater.

In *The Unwritten Law*, we could be in Kafka's Prague as our helpless hero "H" tries to prove his innocence of forever unnamed charges and indeed Santander touches the same nerves as his Czech counterpart. But here that nightmare world is given a bracing shot of modern sexuality and the whole stew then put to political purposes. Santander is a savvy writer and uses mordant wit to skewer his political targets (one of my favorites is the exchange between a torturer and H, who asks, "Why are you hurting me? . . . I've already signed the confession" only to be told that by "babbling everything" before even being touched is bad for the torturers' image. "They're going to think we're not necessary and with all the budget cuts . . .") And while in prison H meets the Professor who explains the workings of the system that has imprisoned them both. It's an explanation that draws on the dramatic events in Mexico's past (such as the slaughter of students by government troupes during the civil unrest of 1968), but it's clear that Santander's targets also include institutions like the World Bank that effect our own political and economic system as well.

We move from the urban landscape of *Law* to the countryside in *The Agronomist* — the first of Santander's plays that I read and my admiration for it only grew after the chance I had to see it on stage in Mexico City. Later, I directed its U.S. premiere in Wisconsin while serving as the artistic director of the Milwaukee Rep. Early in his life, Santander worked as a government extension agent and the play garners part of its authenticity from his experiences. *The Agronomist* is actually the first of a trilogy of plays, each with a separate plot and each examining one of the three pillars of Mexican society, namely the government, the army (*Two Brothers*) and the church (*The Miracle*).

The genre that Santander reinvents in *The Agronomist* is the traditional "corrido," a story told in song that has an honored place in Mexican history as song stories were used to carry news of the Revolution to people who had no access to written accounts of the 1910 uprising. Its skillful use of music, its touching love story and its grotesque Brechtian playfulness in its portrait of the town officials make the play wonderfully entertaining for any audience. But in between, Santander weaves a skillful picture of the Mexican campesino and his complicated world view. Indeed, by the evening's end, Santander has helped the audience to see events through the eyes of the play's peasants. Speaking of the play's ending, it's a unique one and involves, as Holly Hughes puts it, "the two most dreaded words in the American theater: 'Audience participation.'" As a producer, I was pretty nervous about how my Milwaukee audience would react to Santander's innovative ending but I learned to trust my playwright and each night the audience instantly plunged into the spirit of the play's finale. And it was clear from the Milwaukee audience's enthusiastic response to Santander's plays (in the auditorium and at the box office) that his plays have a universal appeal, something I've also seen born out in Canadian productions of his works as well.

Finally, we come to *Mexico, USA*, which Santander announces as a murder mystery. He joins that well-used format with the political thriller and craftily intertwines all that with documentary materials from our own governments often hypocritical attempts at fighting drugs while, for example, illegally aiding the Contras in the 80s. And because of Alvarez's judicious choice of plays for this book, we've gone from urban Mexico to the countryside and now to our own country. Here Riding's "distant neighbors" find themselves cheek by jowl and the results are as explosive as they are unexpected as we follow the fortunes of Santander's heroine, "Ruth Gordon."

Santander is the most generous of collaborators, as I learned through my staging of three of his plays. He is a man with an enormous passion for life and I'm sure that you'll quickly see that exuberance in his writing. He lives in a small traditional village south of Mexico City and though he could live amongst the diversions of that sprawling city, he loves Ocotopec for it's slow pace and old ways. And it's this fierce love of his native country, with which he is so often at odds politically, that fuels his work. We'd sit for hours in the small but comfortable living room of his home (formerly the servants quarters for a nearby hacienda) discussing the complex forces at work in his plays and the rich Mexican history that informs them.

Santander passionately believes theater has a job to do and his plays reflect that. Playwright Amlin Gray tells a story of Santander going to a festival of avant-garde theater. One of the pieces consisted of the curtain going up on a miniature theater. The little box's curtain then went up. A minute passed then the curtain went down, and then the main curtain. Felipe was horrified that the "author" had a theater, had an audience, and presented only emptiness and silence. Santander has a lot to say and doesn't waste a moment of the audience's time in telling his tale. As a result, his plays all move with a Shakespearean sweep with a cast of vivid characters and multiple settings. Should such items daunt prospective producers, I'm happy to report that they're all written to be performed by simple and suggestive means, using medium-size casts who will relish the opportunity to play a variety of delicious roles. Santander's plays have been equally at home on the stage of Mexico's National Theater and off the back of a truck in small pueblos. Let's hope that these terrific translations by Ms. Alvarez means they will also find their way onto U.S. stages where they deserve to be seen.

John Dillon

THE AGRONOMIST

❧

EL EXTENSIONISTA

IN REGARD TO MY WORK

The play opened in 1978, seven years after I had publicly renounced my career as an actor, director, producer and playwright: A career whose first stage could be considered commercially successful, but which I viewed as hollow and limited by the unwritten cultural politics of the country. Three major factors almost dismantled Mexican theater: 1) Theatrical legislation, some of which was carried over from the 19th century. This was used to manipulate productions. The archaic parts of this legislation demanded, among other things, that cats must be on every set (for the rats). It imposed impossible physical requirements — parking lots for each theater and exact placement of toilets. These laws were not enforced except in productions not pleasing to the state (almost all of them). 2) The Technical Workers Federation — an organization totally divorced from the interests and possibilities of theatrical production. Theaters were hamstrung by requirements that imposed standards which often resulted in actors being paid less than those in charge of raising and lowering the curtain — even in theaters where there was no curtain. In one production of Gogols' *The Madman,* for instance, which is a monologue — i.e. with one actor on stage, with no scenery or special lighting, the theater was required to pay 48 technical workers not even chosen by the company. 3) Restrictions from the Actors Union which by the seventies had arrived at a tragicomic level of corruption. I offer a recorded exchange with the Treasurer of the Union during a meeting with 2000 members after the first audit ever organized by the actors:

> TREASURER: Well, yeah, I did build my new house with your union dues — but if it's going to cause such a fuss — I'll give you back your money and let's be done with it!
> (No legal action was taken against this man.)

The actors tried to form a new union but were threatened and stopped by force. Those who persisted were blacklisted in all the principal sources of work: movies, TV and radio. However, censorship was the worst plague of this period. It hobbled the efforts of three generations of Mexican playwrights and actors. McCarthy era Puritanism dribbled down to Mexico, however, in Mexico it became endemic, chronic and crippling. Censorship has lessened to some extent lately — we can watch nude scenes and hear dirty words; we can criticize the government (of other countries) — but politically I don't yet feel the breezes of extraordinary change blowing in our direction. Perhaps now that our old system (the PRI) has fallen, innovations may come, but I don't have many illusions left. Inertia is a bitch.

So, disillusioned by theater in 1971, I returned to my old profession as an agronomist. While fighting to resolve the agricultural problem, I began to write *El Extensionista (The Agronomist),* intending to create a theatrical piece based on my professional experiences in the field. I hoped it would serve as a guide to students from the schools of Applied Agriculture, who were about to begin their fieldwork bringing technical advances to the indigenous communities and peasants. These young people, like my agronomist Cruz Lopez, believed (and their education had taught them) that the problem in the Mexican countryside was technical and not political — as reality would teach them later. Sometimes too much later. I felt it was indispensable that the new generation of agronomists become aware of the situations they would be facing after leaving the classroom. Unfortunately, however, during the ten years the play was "on the boards" (1978–1988) and despite all my efforts, lectures, promotions, appeals to the Secretary of Public Education — we were never allowed to visit one of the country's 1000 agricultural schools. Corruption wasn't limited to the theater.

ABOUT *THE AGRONOMIST*

The structure, philosophy and the very term Agricultural Extension Program were originally copied from the U.S. Agricultural Extension Service Program, which gathered information from research laboratories and university centers and distributed it among the agricultural producers through all the modern means of communication — TV, radio, publications, computers and so on. The idea was magnificent, but it couldn't function in a country whose agricultural structures were isolated, fragmented, impoverished, lacking electricity and credit and with high levels of illiteracy. An Agricultural Extension program á la USA would never reach the majority of peasant-producers who after decades of official pillage and defenselessness had developed their own means of protection — i.e., mistrust, stubbornness, apathy, lying, hypocrisy, maliciousness and go-fuck-yourself-ism.

A much better option was for us to create a system of technical assistance, like the one shown in this theater piece, where the agronomists live with the communities, work side by side with them, share the problems — even those outside their professional concerns — in order to gain the trust of these communities while also generating their own experimental plots to introduce, in a practical way, technical innovations to bring about desired changes.

Instead, perhaps because *El Extensionista* was so successful and provoked innumerable polemics, newspaper articles, threats etc., the government decided to cancel the Cooperative Extension Program, which employed 10,000 agronomists (who are now being used as "firefighters" sent to put out the constant incendiary situations that arise in the countryside, Chiapas being one of them).

TO END WITH AN ANECDOTE . . .

In a place in northern Mexico whose name I don't care to recall — (echoing Don Quixote) — an agricultural engineer (Santander) tried in vain to convince a community of the benefits of using an ammoniacal fertilizer. "No," said the peasants, greatly alarmed. "That fertilizer will freeze our corn." Of course that was illogical since fertilizer has no cooling properties whatsoever. However, I didn't want the discussion to drag on and opted to give a practical demonstration by using my own resources and the plot of land provided for me. Four months later, just at the point of harvesting a magnificent crop — one that would give me the great satisfaction of showing them the error of their ways — the first frost arrived and froze the corn. Here I learned a fundamental truth: Peasants don't always know how to explain natural phenomena, but they understood them much better than we do. No — fertilizers don't have cooling properties, but they do lengthen the vegetative period of corn (the lapse between planting and harvesting) so that the corn is exposed to the first frosts.

CHARACTERS

Cruz	Benito
Chon	Porras
Chon's wife	Balladeer
Mario	Quirino
Jorge	Ismael
Three Prostitutes:	Maximo
Reina, Griselda, and Princess	Manuela
Farm Co-op Members	Nazario
Guera	Cuquillo
Lerma	Boni
Tamez	Montes
Pilo	Innocencia
Dominguez	David
Villalpando	Juancho
Senorita Ramirez	

THE BALLADEER SING

(Accent on the first syllable.)
I come to sing you a ballad
Of Tenochtlen of the flowers
A sleepy town much beloved
Where many people have endured
For many generations.

(Accent on the fourth syllable.)
And you can be very sure that
The sleepy state of the people
Has led some rich men to pillage
The wealth and soul of the village
And engage in exploitation.

(Accent on the first syllable.)
With all the vice and corruption
Neglect led to indifference
Where ever I look around me
Fields are fallow or empty
I see complete devastation.

(Accent on the fourth syllable.)
So in this town I was born in
Most of the orchards are drying.
The ponds and puddles are drying
The corn in fields is drying
The hills, the cattle are drying
The dogs in the streets are drying,
My hands, my throat are drying
The children themselves are crying
Soon we must find salvation.

(Accent on the first syllable.)
So blame the peasants and peons
The workers and their poor families
After all they are nothing
backwardness causes their suffering
They bring their own damnation.

(Accent on the fourth syllable.)
But then the truth of the matter
Can be found really quite simply:
Why break your bones and your back
So some political hack
Will profit from your frustration..

(Accent on the first syllable.)
If you need work from a tractor
You give it oil and fuel it
But for the peasants it's silly
With only tortillas and chile
To have great expectations.

(Accent on the fourth syllable.)
All that we make goes to gringos
Vegetables, fruit and tomatoes
Our cotton and oil are drained
Pipelines of gas and fresh grain
Tequila, fresh fish and romaine.
Our corn and our talent and brains
Are exported again and again
So with what little remains
How do we better our station?

(Accent on the first syllable.)
Now take a look at our children
Who from their tenderest youth
Walk around barefoot and hungry
Dispossessed, listless and angry
Without a good education.

(Accent on the fourth syllable.)
How can this not be the picture.
How can we stop this decline?
If there are more bars and more back rooms
More fancy bordellos than classrooms
Pesos outweigh aspirations.

(Accent on the first syllable.)
If you would think more about it,
You soldier, you mister policeman
That you are also exploited
The workers and peasants destroyed
By this corrupt situation.

(Accent on the fourth syllable.)
So when you beat down the worker
Who complained about his sal'ry,
You are not saving the country,
Only a handful of gentry
Who have defrauded our nation.

(Accent on the first syllable.)
Someday our country will wake up
And rise up to protest injustice,
We'll see we've only been sleeping
Our well being is only our dreaming
Our lives full of deprivation.

(Accent on fourth syllable.)
We'll know this ballad has ended
When our great struggle's begun
To fight against greed and corruption
To stand by our own constitution.
We'll move with no hesitation.

BALLADEER: In this play you're about to see, I'm not one of the characters. I don't even have a name. I'm no one — but you'll see me everywhere . . . No . . . no . . . I'm not the Holy Ghost — that's not it. The truth is — I'm part of everyone, I belong to everyone. I'm the Voice of the People — the voice that doesn't always speak openly — out of shyness, fear, hypocrisy, impotence, apathy . . . the voice that is always there. So you'll see me — especially at the most crucial moments — but I'll be mixed in among the crowd. Sometimes I'll be there as a song, a refrain, a remark, an anecdote — I'm the escape valve for tension and skepticism. I voice the dissension of the country when faced with wrongs that it doesn't know how to redress.

Look, I'll give you an example: Don Quirino Gomez — the official peasant leader *(A fat ugly man enters.)* is in charge of complicating all requests for land; he uses his position to gather money and power for himself and always speaks and makes important decisions in the name of all his neighbors — without ever consulting them. However — it's no use complaining because he was put there by Don Ismael *(Don Ismael enters.)*, our mayor, who in turn was given his position by Don Maximo *(A foreign-looking man enters.)* who is the one here in Tenochtlen who controls all the money and hires and fires our public employees at will.

So faced with this hopeless and helpless situation — the people get even through me. I'm painted on fences telling Don Maximo to fuck off, or criticizing Don Ismael or giving Don Quirino nasty nicknames. *(The three men come forward.)* Sometimes I take the form of open rebellion — that's when my presence is most strongly felt — when the restlessness grows, when the winds of revolution begin to blow . . .

(The curtain opens and we see a revolutionary frieze: A group of peasants begin to argue angrily. Two factions have formed.)

MANUELA: *(With a rifle in her hands.)* If you're with me — follow me now!

NAZARIO: Wait Manuela, we're outmanned. Don't be impulsive! There's too many . . .

CUQUILLO: Shit, who's counting! My men are with you Manuela! We've had enough! *(His men voice their assent.)*

BONI: But we're not even organized!

PILO: We don't even know what to do. *(Murmurs of doubt.)*

MANUELA: We'll surround city hall and demand their return. How much organization do we need for that?!

NAZARIO: At least we should know who and how . . . outline a plan . . .

CUQUILLO: Let's go, Manuela. Forget those shit faced cowards . . .

NAZARIO: Watch who you're calling shit faced coward, you . . . !

(Suddenly they freeze and are silent. There's confusion. The Balladeer takes charge . . .)

BALLADEER: Curtain! Curtain! *(Or "lights, lights" depending on the staging, the curtain closes.)*

BALLADEER: Ah yes, I forgot to tell you that this story hasn't ended yet — since, as you've just witnessed, the country hasn't taken a definitive stand on the matter in question. So now, I'd like all of you to see the entire play from beginning to end. *(Thinks for a moment.)* In fact, I'm going to make you a proposition — we'll start from the beginning and when we get to the scene you've just witnessed, we'll stop, and then . . . listen carefully . . . the rows on this side of the theater will propose one or several possible endings. Then this other side, will discuss them and vote on which will be the ending we stage for you today. All right? *(If there are no questions or objections etc.)*

Okay. Let's begin. Curtain! Lights! Scenery for the opening scene. Let's begin our performance!

(The curtain opens and we find we are in the outskirts of Tenochtlen, a typical Mexican village.)

BALLADEER: We'll begin our story on the day Cruz Lopez, a young agricultural engineer from the city, arrives in Tenochtlen. A Monday afternoon.

CRUZ: *(Stopping Juancho.)* Hey . . . Hey you.

JUANCHO: *(Surprised.)* Yes sir?

CRUZ: I'm looking for a Benito Sanchez . . . where can I find him?

JUANCHO: I don't know. He's probably out in the fields working somewhere.

CRUZ: Yes, but where does he work? *(There's no answer.)* Jesus! How am I going to find him? *(To Nazario who is passing.)*

Hey you! Where can I find Benito Sanchez?

NAZARIO: Who knows. *(He walks faster and exits. Cruz continues his search.)*

BALLADEER: Time passes. It starts to get dark and Cruz hasn't found the information he needs. On top of that — it starts to rain.

(Cruz comes running in and takes refuge under a tree.)

CRUZ: What a shit hole! Am I going to have to kill myself to get anything done here? I've already walked every inch of this place, been bitten by a dog, sank up to my knees in mud and now, this damn rain . . . I bet I get pneumonia. *(He sneezes.)* You see? Shit . . . I shouldn't have come until they delivered my truck, but no I was in such a hurry to get here. *(He sneezes again.)* Now what do I do? *(He sits on a rock and drains the water from his shoes.)* Jesus — my new loafers!

(Manuela appears in a rain cape and begins to urge some animals into a pen. Then she takes some planks and closes the gate so they can't get out. Cruz sees her and goes to help her. She gives him a suspicious look.)

MANUELA: *(Dryly.)* Thanks.

CRUZ: You're welcome *(Seeing that the girl is about to leave.)* Listen, I'm lost . . . I don't know where to go and I've spent the whole afternoon looking for Benito Sanchez — do you know him?

MANUELA: *(After a pause.)* Yes.

CRUZ: And if I ask you where he lives, you'll tell me?

MANUELA: Why do you want to see him?

CRUZ: My God. Thank you. Finally. An actual question. Look. I'm an agricultural engineer, working with the government as part of the Cooperative Extension Program. I've just been assigned to Tenochtlen and they said I should contact Benito. It seems he has some influence with the people here and could help me . . . and uh . . . I've spent the whole afternoon looking for him with not one sighting. Everyone I ask says *(He imitates them.)* Well, he's out working, . . . "out there somewhere" . . . who knows? And now it's dark. *(He sneezes.)* You see?

MANUELA: I'll take you to him if you want.

CRUZ: You bet I do!

MANUELA: I have to clean up here, then I'll take you.

CRUZ: I'll help you. *(They go in the barn and work.)* You know, this isn't a very pretty town. There's nothing here, but hey this is where they placed me — so I'll have to find out what there is to do. People aren't very friendly . . . are you from here? *(Manuela nods.)* Isn't it boring?

MANUELA: No.

CRUZ: So what turns you on?

MANUELA: Turns me what?

CRUZ: What do you like to do . . . for fun?

MANUELA: *(Dryly.)* Nothing.

CRUZ: Don't you like to dance . . . or go to the movies?

MANUELA: There's not much of that around here.

CRUZ: Great — this'll be some life! What would you recommend I do in my spare time? *(Manuela shrugs her shoulders.)* Hey — you know you're very talkative. *(The girl doesn't understand. Cruz doesn't press it. They work.)*

CRUZ: I'm an agricultural engineer. The Government Extension Service sent me. Did I tell you? Yeah well, I'm really proud to be one. I graduated eight months ago, with honors. This is my first job. Took me a while to decide to work, right? It's just that I was trying to find a really cool job with an American oil company. Too bad, I didn't get it. There was only one opening and lots of people applied. I just missed getting it by an inch. They gave it to the guy next to me. *(He laughs.)* It's so cool to work for a Yankee company. They pay you well, they treat you great, plus you can live in the city, dress well and have a good time — not like this one horse town that looks like it's going down the drain no matter what I do. *(Manuela is getting annoyed.)* I mean, I don't want to offend you, but this place sucks. I don't see how a girl like you . . . this place isn't for you you're really pretty . . . *(He takes a good look at her.)* You know, you really are pretty — do they tell you that all the time? You're really good-looking *(Flirting.)* You deserve something better than going around cleaning up after farm animals . . . in the city you'd be a huge success.

MANUELA: *(Furious.)* Look, if you want to see Benito, I'm going to give you some advice — don't talk so much. If I agreed to take you to see him it was because you were so pathetic, all lost and sopping wet, but there's no way in hell I'm interested in the story of your life or in your opinion of our town!

(Silence.)

CRUZ: *(Surprised.)* It's good you don't talk very much.

MANUELA: Okay — let's go. *(They exit.)*

BALLADEER: *(Sings.)* I'll give you three pointers
My city friend
I'll give you three pointers
My city friend
In the country I'll tell you how
Pay attention
Respect tradition
And honor the man with a plow

(Manuela and Cruz arrive at a small adobe house where a small man with a savvy look about him is having supper. This is Benito Sanchez. David, one of his sons, is bringing him food.)

MANUELA: This is it. Knock loud. *(She goes.)*

CRUZ: Thanks a lot. Hey — can I see you again? *(There's no response.)* So you can get on my case again? *(He knocks on the door and David answers.)* I'm looking for Benito Sanchez.

BENITO SANCHEZ: *(Without looking at him.)* Come on in, Mister Engineer, have a taco and a cup of coffee since you're so wet

CRUZ: Thanks. *(He shakes his hand.)* I'm Cruz Lopez, agricultural engineer, the government's sent me to . . .

BENITO: Yes, yes, we'll get to that, for now have a cup of hot coffee it might help you stop shaking.

CRUZ: Thanks. Thanks. Where shall I sit?

BENITO: We've set a place for you here, Mister Engineer *(There's soup, tortillas and coffee.)*

CRUZ: *(Surprised.)* For me? . . . thanks

BENITO: *(To David.)* Go get a blanket. We wouldn't want the engineer to get a cold. *(Cruz is already eating.)*

CRUZ: Listen — how did you know that I was an engineer and that I was coming here?

BENITO: It's a small town. Everyone knows everything.

CRUZ: Did you also know I got lost and stumbled into the swamp?

BENITO: *(Smiles.)* When you're in a swampy area, Mister Engineer, you should follow the donkeys — they never go anywhere where the mud is higher than their hooves. *(They laugh.)*

CRUZ: If you already knew I was lost, why didn't you go look for me or send someone to get me?

BENITO: What? Didn't my daughter bring you?

(Manuela enters with a blanket and a bottle.)

CRUZ: Your . . . .?

MANUELA: *(To Benito.)* Here's the blanket and a jar of mezcal — for the shakes.

BENITO: Leave them over there, Manuela

MANUELA: Well, if you're all set, I'm going to bed.

BENITO: I'm fine. But I don't know if our engineer needs something?

CRUZ: No.

MANUELA: *(She smiles.)* Good night. *(She kisses her father. To Cruz.)* Good night. *(She exits.)*

CRUZ: So she already knew I was lost?

BENITO: We're very shrewd here in this town. Have a drink Mister Engineer! *(Lights out.)*

BALLADEER: After supper, Cruz gave a rather unconvincing account of why he was in Tenochtlen. Benito listened skeptically.

BENITO: *(With irony.)* It's great you've come to teach us how to plant corn.

BALLADEER: Ouch! That hurt! But Cruz, having no experience with the peasants, didn't even notice.

CRUZ: Yes. And not only that, Benito, with your help we can change the peasants' mentality.

BENITO: Change their mentality . . . you mean we have a bad mentality.

CRUZ: *(Smiles.)* What I mean is that they need to learn to think about profit and marketing . . . like businessmen.

BENITO: That would be wonderful . . . God knows the only ones who make money here are the businessmen.

CRUZ: Yes and to get to that point each peasant farmer has to gear himself up to increase production, to become a merchant, an entrepreneur . . . even a corporate man.

BENITO: And you're going to teach us all that?

CRUZ: Well, at least I'm going to try, but of course, first we have to begin by organizing you — that's the first step.

BENITO: So listen — once you've organized us and taught us everything — then we'll be able to be corporate men? I've heard those bastards really make a killing. *(The Balladeer laughs out loud.)*

CRUZ: Well. That would carry capitalization problems and credit . . . but if we have the technical base, who can stop us?

BENITO: Really?

CRUZ: Sure. That's what banks are for. Don't you see, if production is high, the banks earn money. And production always improves if you improve the technology you're using.

BENITO: *(Scratching his head.)* Well, I don't want to discourage you, Mister Engineer, that may happen where you come from — but here credit and technical advancement don't go hand in hand.

CRUZ: But that's not logical. I think you just haven't known how to talk to the banks and they've seen no technical advancements. You know, while I was busy getting lost, I looked around and . . . well how is it possible that nowadays you're still planting corn by making holes with a pointed stick? And how can you possibly plant anything on such a steep incline? . . . and how can you still leave your corn to dry in the sun? *(Benito starts to say something, but Cruz continues.)* We've got to modernize things! Look how you keep your plots of land! I was looking at your dust crop out there on the flats.

BENITO: Dust? We plant beans and corn.

CRUZ: Yes but the way you planted them . . . the only thing that could ever grow would be dust. *(He laughs, sees that Benito doesn't find it funny and becomes serious again.)* Well really things aren't that bad.

BENITO: Mister Engineer, you must be very tired. Go to bed. Benito will make sure all the neighbors know you're here, that the government sent you to help us.

CRUZ: Actually what I'd like is for you to call a meeting, as soon as possible so that I can talk to them. *(The peasants enter with chairs and they gather in the house's patio while Cruz continues.)* If they cooperate with me, there's still a chance that I can save part of your crop, things are bad, Benito, really bad.

BENITO: *(Sincerely.)* Yes, that's the truth, things really are bad.

BALLADEER: But they're not going to get any better with you here, Mister Engineer.

(They all go out to the patio and sit down with everyone. Benito begins the meeting.)

BENITO: Senores, Benito has called this meeting to introduce you all to Engineer Cruz Lopez. *(Applause.)* He's come to tell us how to work the land a little better and to change our pigheaded way of thinking *(Laughs.)* so we can understand things better — like the city people and big business — because these, certainly, are wise and educated people — not half-wits like us. *(The Balladeer laughs and Cruz is becoming uncomfortable.)* The engineer has been sent here by the government, which as always, takes such an interest in us. *(Hostile mutterings.)* This or rather Mr. Cruz Lopez is here, in response to the request we submitted to the authorities, who of course, assured us they would reply immediately. *(Cruz is very uncomfortable with the turn the meeting has taken.)*

CRUZ: What request?

BENITO: Look, Mister Engineer, our problems with land ownership have a long history. The authorities have never wanted to resolve them. Actually it seems they want to complicate them.

CUQUILLO: Of course, what do you think — better fishing if you stir up the river!

GUERA: Yeah, it goes on and on. And never in our favor.

JUANCHO: Hey — we've always known what land is ours. We've owned it forever. But now they come to us with . . . "here's the new boundaries," hell, with a mountain of crap! Somehow the audits always come out in Don Maximo's favor. Imagine! That bandit didn't live here when my grandfather was already plowing this earth.

BONI: They got me too!

BENITO: *(To Cruz.)* With so much paperwork and disorganization, we've got a real tense situation here. Some of my people are desperate. They've begun to take over some of the land on their own.

CUQUILLO: I only took back what they took away from me in the first place.

PILO: Yeah — but cause of you, they're sending their cattle to graze on my land!

(General discussion.)

BENITO: Fine. Okay. Calm down men. We should let the engineer speak — who after all was sent to us by the government — he'll tell us what we should do — right Mister Engineer?

CRUZ: *(Disconcerted.)* Well . . . I . . . don't know. What did the governor tell you?

BENITO: What I just said. That they'd send us news about the land problem . . . and you're the first bit of news we've gotten in a month.

CUQUILLO: Yeah, well I'm telling you — I ain't leaving even if they have sent this engineer fellow!

PILO: Yeah — let the rest of us go fuck ourselves!

GUERA: They shoulda answered us a long time ago — a long time. Jesus! *(General discussion.)*

JUANCHO: Quiet, man, let the engineer tell us what we should do!

CRUZ: *(Doesn't know what to say.)*
Is it that . . . hey are you saying that the government is doing all this on purpose?

GUERA: Christ! Of course!

CRUZ: Who?

CUQUILLO: Who the hell do you think? Don Maximo's people. *(Angry protests.)*

BENITO: All right. Quiet down folks — can't you see Mister Engineer isn't quite up on the situation?

GUERA: Well he should be — if the governor sent him!

CHON: Didn't you say that's who sent him?

CUQUILLO: He should know everything about our problems!

CRUZ: Well I . . . actually I was . . . well what they told me . . . look the truth is I don't know anything. I haven't met the people you're talking about.

NAZARIO: So how're you gonna help us?

PILO: Well what did they tell you?

CRUZ: Nothing . . .

CUQUILLO: This guy's just jerking us around!

JUANCHO: Here we go again — a Band-Aid for a heart attack!

CRUZ: Look. I'm an agronomist. Technically there's lots of ways I can help. I know that the problem you're discussing is very important — but it's outside my expertise. The ways I can help are by telling you what you're doing wrong agriculturally and how to turn the situation around. For example. I've seen that your land is very neglected. You haven't even plowed. That's the worst — I mean it limits the possibilities for retaining moisture. You've got to plow after the harvest, this allows the plants to survive for a longer time during dry spells.

NAZARIO: Sorry, Don Benito — I'm sure what the engineer has to say is very interesting — but I gotta go.

CHON: Me too. I got to see if the pigs laid any eggs yet *(He laughs and the others start to go.)*

CRUZ: Wait, wait. I haven't finished yet.

CUQUILLO: So? Who cares?

CRUZ: Don't leave. At least give me the chance to explain what I can teach you. Benito, ask them not to leave *(Benito is unsure.)* You'll see, if they listen, my work proposal just might interest them. Please.

BENITO: Don Nazario, Cuquillo, Chon. Hold on just a minute, I mean, we're here anyway, let's see what the engineer has up his sleeve. *(Everyone stays but Cuquillo, who stands at the back with his arms folded across his chest.)*

CRUZ: I want to ask you a question. Who owns that piece of land between the slag heaps and the stream? *(Silence. Benito intervenes.)*

BENITO: I believe that's yours, Don Nazario.

NAZARIO: *(Annoyed.)* Yeah, I guess.

CRUZ: I want you to tell me how much corn you expect to grow by acre this year.

NAZARIO: Umm . . . about four hundred kilos.

CRUZ: Wouldn't you like to get, instead, maybe two tons of corn out of there?

NAZARIO: To tell you the truth — no!

CRUZ: What do you mean no?

NAZARIO: Well no.

CRUZ: *(To Benito.)* Look, I don't understand.

NAZARIO: If that's it, can I leave?

CRUZ: *(Exasperated.)* Would you be so kind as to tell me why not? Frankly I don't see the logic in keeping the land so underutilized . . . *(Nazario turns to Benito who makes a sign that he should answer.)*

NAZARIO: That plot of land has yielded up to two and a half tons of corn . . . okay?

CRUZ: What . . . then why?

NAZARIO: Look mister, it's a long story, but I'm going to give you the short version, okay? To get a yield of two and a half tons of corn, you've gotta put money into it, take a risk and why should I? When everything comes out right, they buy our crops at lower prices, they charge us higher interest on loan credit, so in the end we come out the same — so why bother?

CRUZ: What do you mean they lower the price of corn. What about the government price guarantees?

CHON: Man, you can see you never sold corn to the government! *(Laughter.)*

JUANCHO: When it isn't moldy, it's infested, it's chewed by rats, dirty, discolored . . . or it smells bad.

PILO: There's always something wrong with the corn around here — and that costs money.

GUERA: Anyway we always end up selling to Don Thomas, the middleman.

BONI: Although Mr. Thomas and the government are the same thing.

CRUZ: How do you mean — the same?

BENITO: *(To Cruz.)* We think they have an arrangement.

CUQUILLO: You got another little question, engineer?

CRUZ: I have a proposal: I'm going to write down on the blackboard your worst problems — the ones I've seen here, as an agronomist, you understand? Then the idea is that each of you will state honestly what things are going wrong, then we'll discuss it . . . agreed?

GUERA: Sheesh . . . that's gonna be more difficult.

CRUZ: Why? *(Silence.)*

BENITO: It's that at least half of our neighbors here can't read or write.

CRUZ: So then how can you . . . ? *(He becomes agitated.)* Shit!

NAZARIO: Now can we go?

CRUZ: Wait! Let me make one last proposition and then you can go. I propose that you be the ones who give me a technical problem, that you can't resolve yourself, to see if I can help you. Okay? All right. Whoever has a problem raise their hand. *(Everyone raises his hand. To Cuquillo.)* Let's see . . . you.

CUQUILLO: I want you to tell me how to get rid of an infestation that's eating up my corn.

CRUZ: Sure. What genetic traits does it have . . . I mean what is it? Describe it to me?

CUQUILLO: Well, it wears sunglasses. Has a mustache and a belly this big. *(General laughter.)*

CRUZ: Be serious . . .

(Containing himself.)

I'm an agricultural engineer. I received very high grades in school, I did very well. Why not take advantage of what I have to offer? I can teach each of you guys to plant, fertilize, treat a cow, fix a tractor . . .

JUANCHO: Great — but what we're interested in is, where do we get the cow or the tractor or the fertilizer? *(Laughter.)*

BONI: Yeah and I want to know how to keep Don Maximo and his crowd from using up my water!

CRUZ: Well no . . . there's nothing I can do about that.

CUQUILLO: I told you, Don Benito, they've only sent us this baby engineer to sucker us.

CRUZ: *(Loses control.)* I'll give you "baby engineer"! Fuck you, you asshole . . . Let's see about that.

CUQUILLO: *(Also ready to fight.)* Anytime, my itty bitty baby engineer. *(They try to fight. The others separate them. The rest of the peasants start to leave.)*

NAZARIO: We'll see ya, Don Benito.

GUERA: Catch you later.

CUQUILLO: *(Mocking to Pilo.)* You have such soft white little hands.

PILO: Like your sister's.

CUQUILLO: I don't think they're worth shit in the country. *(Laughs and exits.)*

CRUZ: *(To Benito.)* Why don't they try to understand? One thing is technical problems. There I can help you. The others are problems the government has to resolve.

JUANCHO: Oh we're doing just great with you and the government!

CRUZ: *(To Benito.)* You understand me, right? I'm here to give you technical assistance, not to resolve those conflicts you brought up. You know this looks like it's going to be much more difficult than I anticipated. What we have to do is really prepare well for the next meeting — so they don't throw me a curve like they did this time.

BENITO: There's not going to be any more meetings, Mister Engineer!

CRUZ: What do you mean? This was only the first one . . . to sound them out.

BENITO: Benito already told you. We're very bullheaded here — I told you before. If you like, I can call another meeting, but nobody'll come.

CRUZ: So then . . . what do I . . . what am I going to do? I have a contract, a job here that I get paid for . . . you mean that all I can do is throw together my things and walk out? Terrific!

BENITO: *(Sincere.)* Well, that could be the best thing.

CRUZ: *(Impassioned.)* No. I don't agree with you. I'll grab those fuckers by the neck, I'll make them listen to me. They don't know me.

BENITO: *(Calmly.)* The only one who can force them to meet is Don Ismael and his marshals, you know . . .

CRUZ: But you'd come with me to another meeting, wouldn't you, Benito?

BENITO: I think we've done quite enough with Benito — don't you?

CRUZ: You mean — you don't want to learn what I have to teach either?

BENITO: Excuse me being pigheaded and backwards but, in truth, Benito doesn't think you've got much to teach him. Better — go with God, Mister Engineer! *(Lights out.)*

BALLADEER: *(Sings.)* The Indian is stubborn
This you should know
The Indian is very stubborn
This you should know
If you want to convince him
Of something he should know
It's easier to fool him
To stew him
To strangle him
To mangle him
To shoot him
To boot him
To kill him
To hang him
To burn him
Or ruin him
Incinerate,
Consume him
Than to try to make clear
What he doesn't want to hear
What he doesn't want to hear.

(The camp. When Cruz gets to his living quarters, he finds a young solid man waiting for him. This is Mario.)

MARIO: Are you the new agronomist? I'm Mario. I work at the bank.

CRUZ: How're you doing?

MARIO: I heard you had a meeting at Benito's house. *(He laughs.)* How'd it go?

CRUZ: To hell. *(Mario laughs.)* They left me there talking to myself. *(He opens the door.)* Come on in. *(They enter.)*

MARIO: Why'd you go to Benito? You should have gone directly to Quirino — he's the chief of police.

CRUZ: Benito's very respected by these people. He could be very valuable if he wanted to help me.

MARIO: He's a shit — same as all of 'em. I can tell you — they sure showed me when I was going around as the government extension representative.

CRUZ: You were an agronomist here?

MARIO: I started as one. Luckily a position opened at the bank and I quickly got together with Don Maximo. So they gave me the job.

CRUZ: How long were you with the Government Extension Program?

MARIO: About a year.

CRUZ: So you didn't like it?

MARIO: Are you shitting me?

CRUZ: Why not?

MARIO: Believe me — it's much better at the bank, you get more pesos and the work is easier. You don't have to go around trying to shove anything down anyone's throat. I mean, at the bank they either do what you ask or the money's not available. Know what I mean? It all works smooth as silk.

CRUZ: Hey — so can I have your study of the area or some of the results of the Extension Programs? It could help me with my work?

MARIO: (Evasive.) Well, I don't have very much anymore.

CRUZ: Some data on the soil, the climate, some crop statistics.

MARIO: I really didn't have time to do all that.

CRUZ: In a whole year?

MARIO: Look, the truth is, I never really saw myself as an agronomist. I took the job cuz there wasn't anything else, you know what I mean? I knew I'd leave as soon as anything else opened up.

CRUZ: And you didn't have to hand in budgets or reports on what you did? You see — all this stuff is new to me.

MARIO: Yeah. You have to fill out the forms — some printed forms that tell the farmers what to do, what they have to plant and when and all that shit. The bank'll send them to you. All you have to do is give out a hundred forms a week and you've complied.

CRUZ: And the farmers pay attention to these forms?

MARIO: Fuck no! As soon as you turn your back, they tear them up and do whatever the hell they want anyway. But what do you care — all you need is for them to sign on the line — hand in your signed copy — and you're a free man. I could fill out a hundred forms in two hours!

CRUZ: Then on to something else!

MARIO: You got it!

CRUZ: Didn't the supervisors catch you?

MARIO: Are you kidding? They only come when there's a political campaign or to justify a trip somewhere close by — but that's about it. Sometimes the real bigwigs show up — but they warn you a long time before — so you're all prepared with everything in order.

CRUZ: But how can you arrange for all the crops on the plateau to be up and growing? That's really a disaster area.

MARIO: They never go there. I take them to Don Maximo's land — which is fantastic. And right there on the premises we have a big banquet, the booze, some good ass — and everything's taken care of . . . then they go back home.

CRUZ: So they really don't get their hands dirty.

MARIO: You think they're idiots? They always come with a huge group of politicians — representatives of all the Government bureaus — they're not going to traipse out into the fields or criticize each others work — Shit — they only go see what they feel like seeing so they can brag about it later. *(He sees Cruz open his suitcases and unpack his clothes, books, etc.)* What are you doing?

CRUZ: I'm putting my stuff away.

MARIO: What for? Don't tell me you're going to stay here?

CRUZ: Well why have the camp then?

MARIO: Hey — use this as an office, man, or to screw around with one of the native girls — but Jesus — I can't believe you — there's no hot water and you'll freeze your tootsies off at night. *(He sees that Cruz is still unpacking.)* So you're really gonna stay here?

CRUZ: I'm not in touch with these people. I'd like to talk to them a little more, get to know them. I think I can only get to know them outside of work, when they're more at ease, you know?

MARIO: You're going to die of boredom.

CRUZ: Probably. But I really blew it with them today and I'm not about to throw in the towel.

MARIO: It's like talking to a pile of stones.

CRUZ: Could be, but they were right about one thing. They want their land surveyed and registered. Instead of dealing with their problems — the government sent me to distract them or appease them or calm them down.

MARIO: Oh, so they still want their land "regularized."

CRUZ: What do you mean still? The government hasn't resolved a thing. Maybe if I immerse myself in this situation and help them legalize their land holdings, they'll accept me more easily.

MARIO: Don't even think of getting into that shit!

CRUZ: Why not?

MARIO: You'll get your ass kicked. Don't you know the fight is against Don Maximo?

CRUZ: So?

MARIO: Well . . . he's only the most powerful man in the region. He's even more important than Don Ismael — because Maximo is the man who really controls all the centavos here.

CRUZ: And?

MARIO: Look — to make a long story short — if you're on Benito's side — you won't last a month here.

CRUZ: And if I go against Benito — I'll have nothing to do. Great! Look I think the most rational approach is to study the situation. I mean, if Maximo's right . . .

MARIO: He's right.

CRUZ: Benito says his people have always owned this land.

MARIO: They have no documentation. They can't prove it.

CRUZ: Who has any papers around here? It's completely disorganized.

MARIO: Don Maximo. And he's a great old guy. He lets the folks here use his land. And if he really wanted to, he could take it all away in a minute . . . and I hope he does!

CRUZ: Why?

MARIO: Look, Don Maximo really knows how to work this land and he's got the money to do it right. Not those poor jerks who produce less every day. I wouldn't want to even think about what would happen if Don Maximo didn't plant one year!

CRUZ: Well what would happen?

MARIO: Are you kidding? Crop production would fall off so fast in Tenochtlen that nobody'd have a thing to eat! !

CRUZ: I think Benito and his people only eat what they grow themselves.

MARIO: Well them yes — but everybody else. You, me, Quirino, the police chief, the village employees, the bankers . . . we'd all starve to death. *(He looks at his watch.)* Damn! It's five already. Hey, I gotta go. A bunch of us are going out to get laid.

CRUZ: *(Smiles.)* Well, good luck!

MARIO: Look, it's better if you mind your own business. Why don't you come live with me and my buddies. Eh — we've rented a really cool house in the city right downtown. There's eight bedrooms — one's still open. It'll cost you next to nothing . . . and we party! You'd have a great time!

CRUZ: Thanks a lot. I appreciate it, but I'd like to stay here for a while to see what happens.

MARIO: You won't last a week. So when you get tired of driving yourself crazy — you can come live with us — well — if we haven't rented out the room yet.

CRUZ: Sounds great.

MARIO: Be careful, Cruz. Remember one man can't serve two masters. . . . Ciao!

CRUZ: See you. *(Cruz stands there thinking. Lights out.)*

BALLADEER: A month has gone by. In the cantina, people are discussing Cruz's latest failures. *(Discussing.)*

CUQUILLO: So what's this about the engineer visiting you again? Maybe he has romantic intentions *(They laugh.)* I think he likes you.

BONI: *(Embarrassed.)* He brought me some saplings.

CUQUILLO: See?

CHON: Careful, Boni, just don't bend over or he'll plant them so deep your eyes will bug out! *(They laugh.)*

BONI: You guys . . . He just wants me to plant the trees to form a barrier, so the corn doesn't get blown flat by the wind.

JUANCHO: So what'd you do with 'em? Did you plant 'em?

BONI: Hell no — Quirino already wants my property. You think I'd be so stupid as to make it worth more. He'd take it in a minute.

JUANCHO: Cruz came to see us on Monday. There he was walking around and round, measuring out his steps and writing shit down. Then he wanted to go talk to Eduviges and El Chelió — but they'd already heard enough about him and left him there talking to himself.

NAZARIO: Poor devil. We've really shut him out.

CUQUILLO: You can't trust him. He's got some trick up his sleeve.

NAZARIO: No I don't trust him. It's just that he doesn't seem as bad as the rest of them.

CHON: You said the same thing about that guy, the one who came on so strong, giving away all kinds of shit.

PILO: Yeah — he was a student wasn't he?

CHON: He sounded more like Santa Claus — with his "you only have to give me a list of what you want, tractors, sprays, pickers." And there we were complete idiots asking for this, askin' for that and then "poof," we never heard from him again.

NAZARIO: Yeah, but he didn't do us any harm either.

CUQUILLO: Not to you, no, but just go ask Don Andres who had him practically living in his house.

PILO: Yeah — they say Andres even lent him money!

JUANCHO: And he left without a word *(Cruz enters the cantina.)*

CUQUILLO: Oh shit — speaking of the devil . . . Keeps coming back just like ringworm.

CRUZ: *(Pretending not to have heard.)* Good afternoon, gentlemen! *(After a silence.)*

NAZARIO: Good afternoon, engineer.

CRUZ: A small beer please, Guera.

GUERA: Cold?

CRUZ: Yes, please. *(He goes to their table.)* Nothing like a nice cold beer, right?

NAZARIO: Right.

CRUZ: *(Toasts with his bottle.)* To your health, gentlemen!

NAZARIO: And to yours, engineer *(Some of the others answer with gritted teeth.)*

CRUZ: So hey — how's the plowing going?

NAZARIO: Going okay, just fine.

CRUZ: It's getting cloudy — maybe we'll have rain next month.

NAZARIO: Could be. *(An uncomfortable pause.)*

CRUZ: *(Jovial.)* So may I sit down with you guys?

CUQUILLO: *(Getting up.)* Well — I'll be talkin to you.

PILO: Give me lift? I'm going your way.

CRUZ: Aw — don't go. Let me invite you for a drink.

CUQUILLO: *(To Boni.)* Man, all of a sudden it really stinks in here.

CRUZ: Look, I'd like to be your friend.

CUQUILLO: *(Looking at Cruz as he talks.)* — You're being an ass! *(Turns to Nazario.)* Come on Pilo, my boy — let's go. *(They exit.)*

NAZARIO: Have a seat, engineer.

CRUZ: Thanks

NAZARIO: Guera — bring the engineer another beer.

CRUZ: *(Takes out a deck of cards.)* You know how to play cards? Brisca, poker . . .?

NAZARIO: No. We don't like to bet.

CRUZ: *(He shuffles the deck.)* No bets — just for fun.

JUANCHO: Well, Don Nazario — it's getting late.

CRUZ: Wait a second — I have a trick. You see this card? The King of Clubs . . . *(He makes three piles and then moves them around.)* Okay. Which pile is it in? Come on — speak up.

NAZARIO: *(Unsure.)* In that one.

(Cruz turns over the pile and shows him.)

CRUZ: Nope, Not here.

BONI: He got you! *(General admiration.)*

CRUZ: Okay — you Boni. There's two piles left.

BONI: *(He's not sure. He turns to Nazario who nods.)* Well then. . . . in that one.

CRUZ: Oh my goodness, you're wrong too. *(He puts the cards down again. They all look at each other astonished.)* Now you Chon . . .

CHON: *(Laughs.)* This shouldn't be too difficult.

CRUZ: Okay, which pile is it in.

CHON: *(He looks at Cruz and smiles nervously.)* Well it's obvious.

CRUZ: So which one?

CHON: The only one left. *(Laughs.)*

CRUZ: You're sure?

CHON: *(Serious.)* Well, yeah. *(Cruz turns over the cards and to everyone's surprise it isn't there either.)*

CRUZ: Jesus Christ. Not here either. *(Serious.)* Okay — who grabbed it? *(The men look at each other. To Juancho.)* It must have been you!

JUANCHO: Not me!

CRUZ: Let's see . . . right under this hat. *(He removes Juancho's hat and takes out the card.)* So that's where it was!

NAZARIO: Son-of-a-bitch! *(They laugh.)*

BONI: How'd you do that?

JUANCHO: This time you got me good!

GUERA: Hey — couldn't you use that magic to get us titles to our land? *(They all laugh.)*

CHON: That Guera — She can make a joke out of anything!

CRUZ: It's a trick. You want me to teach you?*(General enthusiasm — all gather around to see the trick — even Guera.)* I'm gonna ask you for one favor in exchange.

JUANCHO: Here comes the hook!

NAZARIO: What?

CRUZ: Let me set up an experimental plot on each of your lands.

JUANCHO: Now I really got to go . . . It's very late.

BONI: Right — my old lady must be getting worried. *(They get up.)*

CRUZ: It would be for your own good. I wouldn't need much space.

NAZARIO: I got to go too. Guera — serve the engineer whatever he likes and charge it to my account.

GUERA: Again?

CRUZ: At least tell me, why not.

CHON: *(To Nazario.)* I'll come by for you tomorrow, then?

NAZARIO: I'll be there.

CRUZ: All right. I'll teach you the trick anyways . . . look . . . look how easy it is. *(He follows them to the door but it's no use. Cruz goes back to the table.)* Sssshhhii . . . I blew it again.
(Lights out.)
(In the countryside. Pilo is working the earth. Cruz watches him.)

CRUZ: Quite a wind huh?

PILO: Some.

CRUZ: Doesn't it bother you?

PILO: No. *(The wind blows his hat off. Cruz laughs.)*

CRUZ: Jesus, Pilo, be reasonable — the wind bothers you and it also bothers the plants. It carries off your topsoil, your good soil, the most productive soil — aren't you worried about not having any soil to plant in?

PILO: Well, sure.

CRUZ: So why don't you close up that space in the ravine. That's where the wind gets through . . . look, all you need to do is build up the earth a little, make a mound and plant some trees.

PILO: They already said they'd do that for us.

CRUZ: Build the mound? Who?

PILO: Don Ismael said he'd do it.

CRUZ: When did he say that?

PILO: Two years ago.

CRUZ: And what if he doesn't do it? *(Pilo doesn't know what to say.)* Pilo, making that mound is work you can do for your own good. You're the one who needs it, not the government. Does it seem logical to you to keep waiting for someone else to do something that you can easily do yourself?

PILO: Well, that's what they told us.

CRUZ: So? People don't always do what they say they'll do. Look how the land is. That part over there where the stone's showing through . . . wouldn't it be easy, if you all agreed, to build a mound and reforest the ravine — even if you just did it at the entrance . . . don't you think?

PILO: Well, yeah, that would be good.

CRUZ: Why don't you set them an example.

PILO: I'll see.

CRUZ: Forget this "I'll see" crap. If you agree, I'll bring over the saplings once and for all. *(He goes to his truck.)* And I'll help you build the mound myself. *(Pilo becomes frightened.)*

PILO: No. Well, it'd be better if . . .

CRUZ: Better if what?

PILO: If I wait. It'd be better if I wait.

CRUZ: Look. I'm going to leave you the saplings. Plant them if you want to or not!

PILO: Don't leave them, engineer! They'll dry out!

CRUZ: Let it be on your conscience then — you'll be the one who let them dry out! *(He leaves the saplings and exits furious.)*

BALLADEER: *(Sings.)* There's something you don't understand,
    Perhaps there's a good explanation.
    There's something you don't understand

Consider this realization.
Why would the peasants destroy
Projects they've undertaken?
Why only pretend to employ
Things to improve their situation?

The answer's very simple, "guey"
If you pay close attention.
The answer's very simple, "guey"
About the peasants' intention . . .
If Government projects are ruined
The Government invests again.
It hires the peasants anew
And guarantees work for the men.

(Juancho's plot of land. Cruz is sitting on a stone watching him work.)

CRUZ: You're putting the seed too close together . . . why are you wasting it? You'll get the same results using half of what you're planting — don't you believe me? Look, I know about this stuff. I'm an agricultural engineer — I burned my ass for five years to get this degree. *(He changes.)* Juancho — you seem like a reasonable, sensible intelligent person and I want to propose something for your own good . . . Look — leave a furrow, just one row and plant that one the way I'm telling you — you'll see I'm right.

JUANCHO: Excuse me, Engineer, but there aren't so many furrows that I can waste one.

CRUZ: Well it seems like there's enough seed to waste . . . you stubborn, stone-headed, ignorant, ugly bastard.

(Maximo appears in work clothes. He gets down off his horse.)

MAXIMO: Go ahead, Juancho, sow that row the way the engineer asked you to. I'll pay you for it — I'll pay double what you get for the rest!

JUANCHO: Whatever you say, boss.

CRUZ: *(Surprised.)* Thanks.

MAXIMO: *(Coming closer.)* It's the only way to make them understand. Haven't you learned that yet? You should have learned that by now.

CRUZ: I thought about that — but with whose cash?

(Maximo sits down beside him.)

MAXIMO: Let's look at it through the eyes of experience. *(Juancho watches them as he works. Maximo talks without looking at Cruz.)* I hear you're a hard worker, but you haven't had much success as an agronomist.

CRUZ: That's right. *(He throws a stone.)* It seems like everything I've done is pure and total shit.

MAXIMO: And why haven't you come by to see me?

CRUZ: *(He is surprised and Juancho notices this.)* To see you? Why?

MAXIMO: People usually do around here.

CRUZ: Yeah? and who are you?

(Juancho laughs.)

MAXIMO: I'm Don Maximo.

CRUZ: Oh yes, I've heard of you . . . why should I have come to you?

MAXIMO: Just a minute ago I helped you resolve one problem. Perhaps I could help you with others; other problems a little more interesting than this one. *(He gets up.)* Come by my house. Let's have a drink and talk.

CRUZ: Sure. When I have a minute.

MAXIMO: Good. I'll see you later then. *(He gets on his horse and rides off.)*

CRUZ: *(Looks at Juancho and imitates him.)* "Whatever you say boss!" . . . greedy fuck.

JUANCHO: *(Smiles at him.)* See you later, Mister Engineer!

(Lights out.)

(On the road. Manuela approaches. Cruz catches up to her.)

CRUZ: Manuela! Manuela! I've been looking for you everywhere!

MANUELA: For me? Why?

CRUZ: I wanted to see you, talk to you. Come have a soda with me.

MANUELA: Wouldn't that bore you . . . walking around and around this ugly little town?

CRUZ: Not with you. No.

MANUELA: I'm sorry, but they won't let me. See you.

CRUZ: Manuela! Don't go. Wait. Don't be like that. I don't have anyone to talk to. People flee when they see me coming as if I had leprosy. The other night, before I realized it, I was talking to a cow. *(Manuela laughs.)* Don't laugh, Manuela. It's true. A person can't be alone all the time, I'm like a soul in purgatory . . . wait Manuela. What have I done so wrong that they won't even be friends with me?

MANUELA: Your friends are over there — the other engineers. Go with them, they don't like this town much either. Go with them to the city and have a good time. Don't complicate things for us just because you're bored or have problems. I mean really, it isn't our fault. I never asked you to come here in the first place, and if you leave what difference would it make to me. *(She leaves.)*

CRUZ: But Manuela — it's not like that. Don't lump me in with the rest of them. Manuela! *(Manuela is gone.)* Ssssshhhhhitt. *(He throws a stone at the ground.)* Stupid fucking place. What the hell am I doing here? That's it! That's it! I've had it. I'm getting my things and getting outta here. *(He gets to his door and tries to open it and he can't.)* I hope everything rots. Everything! *(He throws his jacket on the chair. He doesn't know what to do. He begins putting his things away.)* What an imbecile. I'm an idiot to be taking all this shit! *(He takes a gulp of Mezcal and almost chokes.)* Fucking hole. Mario was right. I should pass out forms, pretend I'm working and go have a couple orgies in the city . . . in that eight room apartment . . . with all the hussies I bet they have there. What the fuck am I doing here, playing solitaire? That's it you assholes! Your crops will be infested and then what'll you say? Shit — we never should have let the engineer leave. Let's ask him to come back. yeah sure, Ha! Ha! Let some other asshole help them out. Fuck it if I will . . . fuck it! . . . fuck it! . . . fuck it! . . . fuck it! Fuck it! *(He throws himself down on the bed and cries disconsolately until he falls asleep. He dreams of his mother as we hear a lullaby.)*

LULLABY: Sleep little one
　　Sleep my son
　　Sleep little one
　　Sleep my son

　　Forget your troubles
　　For a time

　　Sleep little one
　　Sleep my son

　　Don't cry no more
　　Don't suffer now

　　Sleep little one
　　Sleep my son
　　Don't try to change
　　The wind or the sea
　　The day will come
　　When you'll have company
　　Sleep little one
　　Sleep my son

And when you awake
You'll see, you'll find
That after the rain
The sun will come
To warm and ease your mind

That after the rain
The sun will come . . .

(It's midnight. Cruz is asleep. We hear laughter and shouts from afar. Mario and Jorge enter with three prostitutes. They're drunk and keep shushing each other.)

MARIO: Is he ever going to be surprised!

JORGE: Here it is.

GRISELDA: We're going to have a party in this pit?

MARIO: Well what did you expect?

REINA: It's cold. Who feels like . . .

JORGE: You sure won't feel cold inside, mama. *(He pinches her. They laugh.)*

MARIO: Sssshhhh. Don't make so much noise.

REINA: This guy's groping me!

JORGE: Oh man, Oh man, I bumped my head! *(Laughter.)*

MARIO: Okay Princess, let me carry you *(He lifts her up.)*

JORGE: *(Pushing on the door.)* Hey — the door's open. That makes it a lot easier.
(They enter quietly. At the same time — Jorge turns on the light and Mario dumps the girl on top of Cruz who wakes up startled. The girl meows and starts acting like a cat. The rest are enjoying the spectacle.)

CRUZ: What's . . . what's this?

MARIO: A surprise party for our new agricultural engineer!

JORGE: All this . . . Courtesy of Don Maximo!
(They set some bottles out on the table. Reina goes and turns on the radio. Mario and Griselda serve drinks and in only a moment a party has been organized in front of the stupefied eyes of Cruz who still isn't quite awake.

JORGE: Lazarus — arise! Go to it, man!
(Cruz struggles to disentangle himself from the girl who has her arms around his neck and is kissing him. The rest are laughing.)

CRUZ: Jesus! I haven't even brushed my teeth!

JORGE: Here — rinse out your mouth with some Martel! *(Laughter.)*

CRUZ: *(While he's throwing water on his face and cleaning himself up a little.)*
I'm totally unprepared. You should have warned me!

MARIO: And lose the chance to surprise you. Forget it!

REINA: *(With a drink.)* You got to catch up with us. Have a drink!
  (The others surround him and give him a drink.)
CRUZ: I don't need much to catch up with you guys. Two drinks and I'm drunk!
JORGE: You said it!
  (He gives Cruz two drinks and Cruz drinks them.)
PRINCESS: That's the way! Come on — let's dance.
CRUZ: Yeah . . . Yeah! *(To Mario.)* Don Maximo paid for all this?
MARIO: Please! Do me a favor and at least tonight — just enjoy life a little.
JORGE: Tomorrow we'll give you all the technical details you want! *(They laugh.)*
PRINCESS: Operation Corruption!
  (She pulls Cruz up to dance with her. Everyone dances. The lights flash giving the party a dream-like quality. To show the passage of time, the music becomes slower and slower until it stops. Finally everyone is lying slumped around the apartment. Lights out.)
  (Morning. Cruz gets up, takes a drink of water and throws some on his face. The others are still sleeping. Cruz goes to Mario and tries to wake him.)
CRUZ: Mario . . . Mario! *(He shakes him.)* Wake up!
MARIO: Wh . . . what's happening?!
CRUZ: I'm leaving.
MARIO: Great. Have a good trip. Good-bye. *(He goes back to sleep.)*
CRUZ: Mario! *(He takes his covers off.)* You don't get it. I'm getting out of here. I'm leaving Tenochtlen. I don't want to work for the Government Extension Program anymore!
MARIO: *(Stammering.)* Yeah well — okay what's got you so riled up?
CRUZ: I'm a failure!
MARIO: Ay, that's bad. Couldn't get it up for the princess?
  (Cruz is getting mad. Mario laughs.)
CRUZ: I've failed with everything and everyone!
MARIO: Look, if you let me go back to sleep, I'll tell you some good news, okay?
CRUZ: Okay.
MARIO: None other than Don Maximo wants you to come to his house tonight. He liked you. Now everything will change for you . . . man . . . plenty of pesos!
CRUZ: No. You didn't understand. It's my career, my profession that I've failed at.
MARIO: Don't give me that shit.
CRUZ: No. Really.
MARIO: But now you can do whatever you want. With Don Maximo's blessing, every door will spring open for you — wait and see.

CRUZ: But Maximo's gotten rich exploiting these people and these are the people I think my work should serve!

MARIO: *(Mocking.)* You're talking like a fucking demagogue! Do you really believe that Don Maximo could give a shit about these fucking people?! They're pathetic.

CRUZ: Well he hasn't done much for them.

MARIO: Be real. He's opened up jobs for them — where they could earn some cash. Without him — this town would have been bankrupt years ago.

CRUZ: It's almost bankrupt now.

MARIO: And if it wasn't for Don Maximo lending them all money — it'd be that much worse.

CRUZ: Instead of throwing money at them, he should give them a chance to live by their own work!

MARIO: They don't want to. Haven't you seen that? They don't want to work! They'd rather go around begging in the cities!

CRUZ: What do you mean, they don't want to work? What about all those guys who go to the States? Up there people think our peasants are the best workers they've ever seen. Especially in manual labor.

MARIO: Don't talk to me about "The States" We're talking right here. You tried to help them and what happened? What have you done for them?

CRUZ: *(Embarrassed.)* Nothing, But that's because I'm an idiot.

MARIO: That's not why and you know it. And just so you know the same thing's happened with Don Maximo. He tried to help them but it's no use. They won't do anything. You can't get blood from a stone.

CRUZ: I don't think the answers to their problems are going to come from people like Don Maximo.

MARIO: Look — let's not talk about all that class struggle shit right now. Do you know how to make the situation better for these people?

CRUZ: I've got some ideas, my program for regional development.

MARIO: The one you talked to me about?

CRUZ: Yes.

MARIO: And you're convinced that if this program is put into action Benito and his people will reap the benefits?

CRUZ: Well, I think so . . .

MARIO: Okay, then let me suggest something: Take all this to Don Maximo and if he doesn't help you get this program going, just the way you want it, exactly like you've planned it out, then tell him to go fuck himself and be done with it. What do you think?

CRUZ: *(Undecided.)* I don't know. I don't get a good feeling about this guy Maximo.

MARIO: So . . . forget it! If you're going to judge people only by what other people say . . . and if you don't even give them a chance to prove themselves — there's no sense in even talking! *(Mocking.)* It ain't like Don Maximo's the boogey man!

CRUZ: All right. All right. I'll go see him. There's nothing to lose . . . I don't think. *(Lights out.)*

(Don Maximo's elegant, modern and comfortable residence. Maximo and Don Ismael are talking to each other in a very dry formal manner. Don Ismael seems quite perturbed.)

MAXIMO: Unfortunately, Don Ismael — I can't afford to have friends. My interests are too widespread.

ISMAEL: Our situation is critical — if we can't get another loan we won't be able to pay the police or any other town employees — and without them, without their support our government may fall. There are a lot of internal pressures. As you're well aware, the town was handed over to me in disastrous shape.

MAXIMO: I understand your problems, but you also have to understand my position. The town already owes us too much money — and really, I don't see how or where they're going to get money to pay me back.

ISMAEL: Look — we know you've had trouble with your cattle because of the drought . . .

MAXIMO: This has been a bad stretch . . .

ISMAEL: Well we've been lucky enough to discover some underground streams that, according to the Office of Irrigation, are quite abundant . . .

MAXIMO: Streams? . . . where?

ISMAEL: Next to that bare hill. It'd be easy to build an aqueduct and steer some of the water your way . . . in exchange for dismissing our debt.

MAXIMO: The water pressure's good?

ISMAEL: More than you'd think. Do you want us to send you the results of our technical study?

MAXIMO: Please do and the contract conditions. If the situation is really as you stated, I'm sure we can come to an agreement.

ISMAEL: I'll send it to you immediately.

MAXIMO: *(Getting up.)* Good. As soon as I receive it and have had a chance to look it over, I'll get back to you.

ISMAEL: *(Cold.)* Good. Have a good evening.

MAXIMO: *(Cold.)* Good-bye. *(Ismael leaves and Cruz enters.)* Well, well, engineer, come on in . . .

CRUZ: Those are some tractors!

MAXIMO: You like them? I just bought 'em . . . the key to getting good crop yields is to use only the best technology — I wish everyone could understand that.

CRUZ: It's easy to understand . . . but . . . not so easy to afford. And what about unemployment? More machines, less hands.

MAXIMO: So how's your work with the farmers going? They treating you better?

CRUZ: No. And I think . . .

MAXIMO: Your problem is you've done everything backasswards. To begin with, you should never ask those people what they want to do; you tell them what they have to do.

CRUZ: Sure — I'll just go grab them and beat them into compliance.

MAXIMO: That's where you should have come to me. I've already been through that and I know how to handle them, how to make them do things the way they should be done . . . of course, for their own good.

CRUZ: You mean force them to let themselves be helped?

MAXIMO: Exactly. It's the only way. I understand your anxieties — but I hate to see you wasting your time like this.

CRUZ: Well yeah.

MAXIMO: Engineer Cuevas, told me, Mario . . . that you have quite interesting agricultural plans for this region.

CRUZ: I have something.

MAXIMO: And that this plan could substantially increase our production.

CRUZ: It's rather a crop diversification plan.

MAXIMO: Sounds good.

CRUZ: I've been studying the soil here and I think the land is being wasted by planting only corn. I'm convinced we could get an excellent yield by planting cotton . . . especially in the valley.

MAXIMO: Cotton? No one's ever planted that here. Do you think it'd grow?

CRUZ: Yes! There's a variety that produces a good quality and a high yield of fiber. It's been tested in many climates very similar to ours here, the same altitude, and latitude. The soil depth is ideal and the dry periods here fit very nicely with its growing cycle. The only limitations we'd have would be water and credit.

MAXIMO: I don't have those limitations. I have money and water.

CRUZ: Yeah — but I'm not talking about you . . . My plan could help these people who, after all, are the worst off.

MAXIMO: *(Smiles.)* I understand. You're very reasonable. I wish we had more young men who think like you do. But then, how would you see my role in all this?

CRUZ: You'd be the one who'd help us find water and credit.

MAXIMO: Good God!

CRUZ: Mario says you want to help Tenochtlen and I'm giving you a chance to put your money where your mouth is.

MAXIMO: *(He laughs.)* You drive a hard bargain! Let's see . . . How can we do this? Credit is no problem . . . easy to get. But water? I can't guarantee you more than my quota allows.

CRUZ: That'd be enough!

MAXIMO: What about me?

CRUZ: You could plant seasonal crops. Everyone would love that and you'd improve your image.

MAXIMO: *(Joking.)* Aren't you pushing your luck just a little?

CRUZ: I mean — you're already rich. Give us this opportunity to break even for a change or to earn a small profit.

MAXIMO: Hmmm. I'd sow corn and beans and you could plant cotton. Would you help me?

CRUZ: Of course!

MAXIMO: All right — Done! You can count on the water.

BALLADEER: Wait. Hold on!

This is an extremely important decision. We should be really clear about this moment. So let's hear it again.

(The scene is replayed as follows.)

MAXIMO: I'd sow corn and beans and you could plant cotton . . . would you help me?

CRUZ: Of course.

MAXIMO: All right — done! You can count on my water.

CRUZ: I need this in writing. So nothing falls between the cracks — okay?

MAXIMO: You're very sharp. Agreed then, in writing.

CRUZ: Could we get together with Lerma, the engineer from the Irrigation Department and formalize this agreement as soon as possible?

(The tone here is farcical. Lerma appears in the doorway. As each person is mentioned, he enters and greets Don Maximo with a handshake and a big smile. Then they proceed to their chairs and sit quietly and wait.)

MAXIMO: I'll ask him to come talk with us.

CRUZ: And the credit? Are you sure the bank will back us up?

MAXIMO: I think so. It's only a matter of meeting with Tamez who's a good friend of mine.

CRUZ: We'll have to dig some canals and build some retention holes.

MAXIMO: We'll call in Montes.

CRUZ: Commercialization is very important. We need to get a guaranteed price and distribution. I don't want us to have to go through middlemen.

MAXIMO: Dominguez can arrange that.

CRUZ: The Agrarian Reforms — We want a written guarantee about land ownership. And this can't be left dangling until it's time to bring in the harvest either!

MAXIMO: I'll call in Villalpando.

CRUZ: Oh yeah — and a representative from the Department of Agriculture so we have his approval and technical aid.

MAXIMO: Let's talk to Porras and for public relations, we'll get ahold of Mrs. Ramirez.

CRUZ: Do we need her?

MAXIMO: Yes. I've worked well with her before, and with her body . . . well she has a way of being able to communicate with these people in a way they understand. *(Mrs. Ramirez enters. Everyone at the meeting is happy to see her.)*

CRUZ: We should invite a representative from the group of peasants, to make sure we can count on them.

MAXIMO: Fine. We'll call in Quirino. *(Quirino starts to enter but stops as he hears what Cruz has to say.)*

CRUZ: No. I'd rather call Benito Sanchez. People don't like Quirino very much. *(Benito appears and is about to enter when he hears Maximo.)*

MAXIMO: But Quirino is the official representative. *(Quirino pushes past Benito and is ready to enter when Cruz's voice stops him.)*

CRUZ: But Benito really represents the peasants.
(Benito gets Quirino out of the way and stands in his place.)

MAXIMO: Benito's a troublemaker. We'll only have problems with him. *(They change places again.)*

CRUZ: If we convince Benito, he's the one who can convince the rest of them to participate in this project.

BENITO AND QUIRINO: So? Which one do you want?

MAXIMO: I'll tell you what. Let's invite both of them. Agreed?

CRUZ: Agreed.
(Both men enter and sit down at the meeting.)

MAXIMO: Okay, now, I think it would be best if Don Ismael presents your ideas initially since he's the highest official in Tenochtlen. Don't you agree? *(Cruz is about to say something.)* I'll speak to him beforehand. He'll be completely briefed on your plan before he comes to the meeting. He'll present himself as the one who's backing you on this!

(Ismael enters hurriedly and everyone stands. He asks them to sit down and then addresses them.)

ISMAEL: Gentlemen — we're here today to analyze a program that our engineer Lopez has presented to me, one which I consider to be of great importance — especially since it reflects our current political spirit. His program defines quite clearly the problems in the countryside. Agricultural production has sunk to a disastrous level. There's hunger in Tenochtlen and I am deeply pained that those of us who are responsible on one level or another have let things decline so far. How can we talk about a serene happy village when every day there is less and less food. How can we broach the subject of a prosperous town when children are walking barefoot in the streets; how can we even talk about social justice when justice hasn't reached each and every one of our citizens! *(Applause.)* Please, gentlemen, this isn't a political speech. I'm trying to present a realistic analysis of our situation. And I believe, despite the problems I've just mentioned, this isn't the time to tear our clothes and put ashes on our faces. It's time we act united in an effective way, organizing a true alliance to help production so that we can resolve our most urgent problems as soon as possible. We can prevent the shame of our men having to look outside of Tenochtlen for work, work which we could provide if we all act together now in good faith.

QUIRINO: I am profoundly moved, Mister Mayor. My life has been changed forever in this most sublime moment which you have so glorified with your words.

ISMAEL: Jesus, Quirino! Let's not use this moment for beautiful rhetoric or to impress anyone.

QUIRINO: I . . . I'm . . . I'm sorry sir.

ISMAEL: I'd like to ask Engineer Lopez to come up here and lay out his plan for us.

BALLADEER: All right, Cruz!
Give it to 'em! Give it to 'em!
Give it to 'em!

CRUZ: This plan has two fundamental objectives: a social objective which will try to resolve the unemployment and low income levels we find in agriculture — both of which lie at the root of many other problems — like malnutrition, pollution, illiteracy . . .

AD LIBBED VOICES: It ain't so easy.

It's not our fault.

We're broke!

You're way off!

Increase production. That'll do it!

Yeah, production is what's important!

EVERYONE: We must increase production! We must increase production! We must increase production!

ISMAEL: Please everyone. Let the engineer continue.

CRUZ: The second objective is to sell, outside of Tenochtlen, the surpluses we get so we'll have money to buy what isn't produced here.

PORRAS: That is an excellent plan!

ISMAEL: Especially now that Tenochtlen is drowning in debt because of outside expenses.

BENITO: Excuse me sir, but when you refer to Tenochtlen drowning in debt — you must be referring to you and your cronies, no?

ISMAEL: I'm talking about everyone. We all share in the debt.

BENITO: Why us? We never loaned nobody any money.

ISMAEL: Our bank has loaned you money — and in order to do that, we, in turn, also had to ask for a loan.

BENITO: We paid you back. So you should already have paid off your debt too.

ISMAEL: It's not that simple. Not everyone has paid up.

BENITO: Well then — define the limits of responsibility and those who still owe, should pay . . . That's one for the book — you borrow money and I have to pay it . . . are you shitting me?

ISMAEL: I acquired the debt in your name, with your consensus.

BENITO: *(To Cruz.)* With our what?

CRUZ: *(Whispering.)* With your permission.

BENITO: What permission?! We didn't even know about it!

QUIRINO: Don Ismael can't consult with us on every little decision he needs to make. We gave him our power and our trust when we elected him Mayor!

BENITO: When I elected Don Ismael?? . . . Don Maximo put him there. Screw that!

QUIRINO: Please, I beg you show more respect for our highest elected official.

BENITO: Oh yeah. Sure! After he told us he got us in debt for our own good!

MONTES: It wasn't even Don Ismael who caused the debt . . . it's been carried over from before.

BENITO: No . . . don't even begin with that shit . . . where we end up not even knowing who's screwed us or from which end.

MONTES: What's happening is that you guys don't want to look at the expense to the government of all the services you get.

BENITO: You're right, I have no idea what services I'm getting. Maybe you'd like to enlighten me.

MONTES: With pleasure — the dam, the canals, the wells . . .

BENITO: Oh right. Yes, what a benefit! All those only affect the properties of Don Maximo's people.

VILLALPANDO: Sure cause you people rent and sell your land . . . like with that farm "El Olote."

BENITO: Right. With Olote — you didn't begin your work until the owners were dying of hunger and had to sell it to put food in their mouths. The same thing happened with the "ejido."

MONTES: That's a very serious accusation!

BENITO: Take it any way you want. Benito stands by what he says!

PORRAS: Well I can give you some examples of money spent on you! Last year we bought a truck for Engineer Cuevas so he could get around to all of you and give you technical assistance!

BENITO: Oh that's what it was for. And all this time, Benito couldn't figure out why so many girls were riding around in it . . . it was for technical assistance! And you know — there's three of those girls with bellies out to here from all that technical assistance! *(Laughter.)*

ISMAEL: Please, gentlemen, you're wasting time with useless arguments that lead nowhere. It's true, that in the past, there have been certain irregularities.

BENITO: Actually, they've been quite regular!

CRUZ: Please, Benito.

ISMAEL: And that's what we're trying to change. Please, Lopez, continue.

CRUZ: I'm going to simplify it. We need to plant cotton in the valley. There's two varieties that have already been tested. I have here the results of the study. Cotton would really increase the earnings of you farmers.

BENITO: Ha! I can see it now!

CRUZ: *(To Benito.)* The profit from cotton is about five times that from corn. On the other hand, it's a crop that's labor intensive, it requires a lot of care, by hand, especially in the harvesting — so it would entail more work for your people.

BENITO: They're not my people! They're not my property!

CRUZ: Also part of the processing could be done here in Tenochtlen. That would certainly bring a major economic boom that would help everyone in this town. Okay, now a program of this magnitude would require the support of everyone here and all the dependents that you represent in order to succeed. And on the basis of written contracts that are very specific. *(Murmurs of distrust.)*

AD-LIB VOICES: A written contract?

Your distrust is offensive to me. You'd doubt my word?

I can't make a decision just like that!

We've got to look at the results of that study!

An exhaustive analysis.

This needs a lot of planning! A lot!

Right, planning!

ALL: Planning, planning, planning!

MAXIMO: Lopez's plan has my total support.

(General confusion.)

ISMAEL: And I think the best thing would be to implement this program as soon as possible!

(Arguments among the officials. They make a decision.)

VILLALPANDO: Considering the actual conditions here in Tenochtlen, and the desperate need for investments to get us out of this economic abyss, we'll consider this program. Even without a written plan, we can see it will allow us to begin some work for the public good that, soundly supervised and evaluated, will give us, unilaterally, the co-efficients we'll need to take action against the overwhelming inflation, wiping out substantially the limitations in our community caused by vertical restrictions which geometrically impact on our *(He loses his place.)* on our, well, what I mean is this program can count on our unconditional support! Ay! *(They shake each others hands.)*

ISMAEL: What about you, Benito?

BENITO: Benito doesn't trust this program.

AD-LIB VOICES: Always negative!

You just have to be uncooperative!

Unpatriotic!

You're doing it just to go against them!

(They sing and dance.)

Negative as always

No hope, no patriotism

Creating always problems
With your civic negativism

Stubborn and aggressive
Overly possessive
Perhaps then your complaints
Are backed by communism
Are backed by communism
Are backed by communism . . .

MAXIMO: Enough . . . quiet!

(Everyone quickly takes their seat.)

ISMAEL: Why don't you have faith in this program, Benito?

BENITO: Benito is thickheaded, he don't know how to explain things . . . and it causes him a little trouble to see how, all of sudden, everyone is so interested and so committed to better the situation for those of us who are the worst off. Truthfully, Benito don't believe it, even if you order it yourself, sir.

ISMAEL: I don't blame you for thinking that way, Benito. We've failed you so many times before and for that I ask your pardon. However, I insist that this time you have nothing to lose and a lot to gain.

BENITO: Nothing to lose? You call this food we eat nothing! I still remember when you convinced us to plant garlic. We spent a whole year gagging on garlic because we couldn't sell it!

PORRAS: There was over production and the market fell.

BENITO: So why'd you tell us to plant it in the first place?

PORRAS: These things happen, there's no way to foresee every trend.

TAMEZ: The production figures were skewed.

VILLALPANDO: Our statistical base was deficient.

BENITO: Maybe it was the winds . . . but that year there was real hunger in Tenochtlen.

MAXIMO: It'll be different this time. There'll be a guaranteed price for the cotton.

LERMA: And we'll guarantee a buyer

BENITO: Our only guarantee that we'll have something to eat is to plant corn and beans.

CRUZ: But, Benito, with the money you get from selling cotton you'll be able to eat meat and eggs and milk too!

BENITO: At least you can eat garlic. Cotton clumps in your belly and makes you constipated.

CRUZ: They're going to guarantee you the price and the sale in writing!

BENITO: Papers mean nothing to us. Some of us can't even read. We believe in a man's word — but to tell you the truth, your words have never meant anything to us. *(He stands.)* So if there's nothing more you have to say . . . *(He starts to leave. Ismael stops him.)*

ISMAEL: Before you go, Benito — I want you to think a little. This cotton program will be done with or without all of you because it's desperately needed. So that decision is already made. Now cotton is expensive, and once we give credit to those who are going to plant cotton, there might not be much money left for corn and beans.

BENITO: *(Scratching his head.)* What bastards!

ISMAEL: It's a difficult decision. So I recommend that before you make it, discuss it with your people.

BENITO: *(To Cruz.)* And you — what do you think?

CRUZ: I think they're right. *(Benito smiles ironically.)* You'll see in the long run this program will benefit everyone.

BENITO: Well, Benito's leaving and fuck all of you!
(He leaves. Lights out.)

BALLADEER: *(Sings.)* People have learned how to use
their bank loan to gain a foothold
Half for seed and then manure
Insecticide to keep things pure
And half to feed the household . . .

And this is the situation
Where Benito sees only defeat.
If they don't plant their cotton
They'll remain poor and forgotten
With no money left to eat.
And there really is no choice
But the government's request.
So they set to work at last
To do what they've been asked
Without joy or eagerness.

But with no eagerness.

CRUZ: *(Joyous, with great enthusiasm.)* Move the tape more to the right. More! More! You've got to get it at an angle! There! Okay, set the marker! The water has to pass through here so that it's well distributed. All right, you guys keep on . . . but come on . . . with enthusiasm — you don't seem to get that it's your own business

(As soon as he walks away, the farmers rest.)

CRUZ: *(In another place.)* No. No . . . you have to make the borders higher. Let me show you! *(He raises a border. He jokes around.)*

And you guys — what are you staring at. Go do it yourselves! With spirit, with enthusiasm. Soon you'll be rich! *(He goes.)*

CRUZ: *(He brings in another group of farmers who follow him reluctantly.)* What do you mean it's time to go? You still have all these rows to go. Come on, I'll help you. It's our chance to show them what we can do . . . and do it well! It's your money that's on the line! Let's dig in, all night if we have to! *(Lights out.)*

BALLADEER: *(Recites.)* With his great spirit
and valor
Cruz fired the people's
enthusiasm
But despite breaking their backs
in the fields
The winds of fraud and
betrayal blew in

Winds of fraud and betrayal
blew in.

CRUZ: *(To Chon who grows pale when he sees Cruz.)* How deep are you planting that?

(He scratches the earth and doesn't find any seed.)

It shouldn't be more than five centimeters deep. You see? You've lost it. Here — give me a little of that seed.

(Seeing that Chon hesitates, Cruz sticks his hand in the sack of seed and pulls up a handful of something that isn't seed.)

And this? What's this? What are you putting in the ground? This isn't the seed I gave you . . . why are you planting this? Answer me! *(He grabs Chon by his shirt and pulls him towards him.)* Don't you know that if you don't sow you won't have a harvest? Where's the seed? Tell me where the seed is or I'll push your teeth down your throat!

CHON'S WIFE: Don't hit him! We changed it for corn.

CRUZ: What?

CHON'S WIFE: We had nothing to eat.

CRUZ: Don't you see that this way you'll have even less? *(To Chon.)* Who changed it for you.

CHON: The guy at the distribution center. He gave us two sacks of corn.

CRUZ: I can't believe it! Shit! That was special seed — it's worth ten times what you got. Do you see how they take advantage of you!

CHON'S WIFE: You can't think well when you're hungry.

CRUZ: You should have taken out credit!

CHON: Credit? Sure . . . what credit?

CRUZ: The credit we secured from the bank.

CHON: Mmmm. They gave us the seed, some buckets of pesticide and those boxes over there . . . but money? . . . you must be joking.

CRUZ: It was authorized two weeks ago. Why, what did they tell you?

CHON: Well . . . that they had no record of it.

CRUZ: Fuck me! And why didn't you guys tell me? *(Chon shrugs his shoulders.)* I'll be right back! *(He leaves furious.)*

(In the bank's office, Mario is waiting on a group of cooperative farmers who look very worried.)

MARIO: *(Very professional.)* Unfortunately, there's no way the bank can make a loan as large as you requested. The cotton program has left us virtually without any funds.

COOPERATIVE FARMER: *(Anguished.)* It's that if we don't drill the well now we won't have water for our animals.

COOPERATIVE FARMER 2: You promised us, right before we went to buy the drills that you'd finance them.

MARIO: You're right. That's what I intended to do. But, you know how it goes — Man proposes and God disposes.

COOPERATIVE FARMER 2: Jesus Christ . . . what are we going to do now?

COOPERATIVE FARMER 1: We'll have to sell our stock.

COOPERATIVE FARMER 3: And all the money we invested in the installations? We'll lose everything!

COOPERATIVE FARMER 4: What the hell did we form this cooperative for then?

COOPERATIVE FARMER 3: Just to lose what we already had.

MARIO: Look — I really shouldn't tell you this as a bank employee — but there's someone who can help you.

COOPERATIVE FARMER 2: Who, sir?

MARIO: Don Tomas Urrutia — who owns the pharmacy. That old man has a lot of money and I know he makes loans. The only thing is he charges a high interest, but in an emergency like yours.

COOPERATIVE FARMER 1: Can you tell us where to get in touch with him?

MARIO: I'm writing it down for you now. Go see if you can arrange something . . . and if not we'll try to find another way. Believe me I really want to help you.

COOPERATIVE FARMER 4: So let's go right now. *(They go towards the door.)*

MARIO: Go, go and God Bless you. *(They leave. Mario picks up the phone.)* Hello. Don Tomas? I'm sending over some clients. I think it'll work out swell. Eh? Well ask for ten percent a month. Yeah — so they'll get it down to nine percent which is still very good. Yes. Sure. So when you make the deal with them, just fill out the loan form and send for the money — I'll have it all here waiting for you. Yeah. Yes. Sure. *(Cruz enters.)*

CRUZ: I'd like to know why you haven't given cash credit to the peasants?

MARIO: Ah — how you doing, Cruz. I'll be right with you. *(He starts to leave, but Cruz grabs his arm.)*

CRUZ: No. You'll answer me right now. The credit should have been available three weeks ago.

MARIO: Credit? I already gave them almost all of it.

CRUZ: Yeah — seed, fertilizer . . . but you haven't given them one cent so they can eat. They've already begun to exchange what you gave them for corn.

MARIO: Take it easy, Cruz. Don't get excited, those people would have done it anyway. They always do.

CRUZ: Of course. And if I were in their place, I'd do the same!

MARIO: Look, look Mr. Pissed-Off, what do you want us to do?

CRUZ: What are you talking about! Give them money so they can eat. That's as clearly outlined in our contract — so we could stop something like this from happening.

MARIO: *(Confidential.)* Look — there's not enough money. You know with all the campaign stuff, it cost us a lot of dough — you know how it is and now . . . we've run out.

CRUZ: I don't give a damn about the campaign. What I want to know is how we're going to resolve this problem!

MARIO: Jesus, Cruz — don't make mountains out of molehills — you're going to create hard feelings.

CRUZ: We'll talk about that later. Right now, we have got to have the money!

MARIO: Look. I'm going to give you some advice, that is if you really want to solve the problem for these folks. Why don't you go see Don Tomas Urrutia — the pharmacy guy. He's loaded — but he'll loan money immediately which is what you guys need. He's going to want to charge a really high interest rate — but you can argue him down. I mean, the cotton crop is a very profitable crop and you can afford this type of expense to get it going.

CRUZ: *(Controlling himself.)* Mario, I didn't come here so you can send me to some usurious money lender who'll rob us blind. There's a written contract which the bank promised to respect and I'm going to make them respect it!

MARIO: OK! Wait let me see what I can do . . .

(Mario gets on the intercom and calls various times, the light goes on in Tamez's office where we see him seducing his secretary. Very reluctantly he answers the phone.)

MARIO: Engineer Tamez?

TAMEZ: What's going on?

MARIO: I'm sorry to disturb you, sir, but Cruz is here with me. He says that the farmers in the cotton program need money.

TAMEZ: Look, Cuevas, don't bother me with that shit!

MARIO: Yes, sir. I told him that — that we've requested the funds and that it's only a matter of time. Only, sir, Cruz is extremely worried.

TAMEZ: And what the hell do I care about that?

MARIO: Yes. Yes. I'll tell him. You're very worried too.

TAMEZ: What's the matter with you Cuevas — why are you talking like that? Are you nuts?

CRUZ: Tell him I want to talk to him!

MARIO: It's that . . . it seems Cruz wants to talk to you.

TAMEZ: I have nothing to say to that idiot! *(Cruz hears this and starts towards Tamez's office.)*

MARIO: I know that sir, but unfortunately, I think he's already heading your way. *(He's going there now.)*

TAMEZ: What? What kind of ineffectual wimp are you? The only reason I keep you there is to . . . *(The door to his office bursts open and Cruz enters — despite the efforts of the receptionist and her assistant to restrain him. Everyone stands there embarrassed at the scene. Lights out.)*

BALLADEER: The credit was finally arranged — although not quite within the proper time line. But the conflict with the bank was only the beginning of Cruz's encounter with layer upon layer of corruption in Tenochtlen.

(In the irrigation offices Cruz argues with Jorge.)

CRUZ: What do you mean there's no water. The agreement clearly specifies . . .

JORGE: Agreements don't make it rain! The extended drought has lowered water levels even more than . . .

CRUZ: Fuck the drought! There's always been droughts here!

JORGE: Don't get so upset, Cruz — it's not my fault. Have I ever failed you before? Haven't I given you water unconditionally for the five prior irrigation's.

CRUZ: Yes but . . .

JORGE: Of course I did because there was water! But it's gone. What do you want me to do?

CRUZ: Plan better! When you make a commitment to a project with so much at stake . . . you need to guarantee.

JORGE: The statistical data they gave me was screwed up. It was wrong.

CRUZ: Funny all the statistics in Tenochtlen seem to be very conveniently "wrong"!

JORGE: Look since I don't have a direct connection to God — I don't see what else I can do for you.

CRUZ: I don't want anything else! All I want is for you to honor your commitment. You know that this is the most important irrigation phase. Without this one — there's no harvest, no crop. We'll lose our entire investment. Maybe you'd pay attention if we all came down and set your office on fire.

JORGE: *(Laughs.)* Don't push it, Cruz. That's not doing you any good. *(Serious.)* I swear to God, you're looking for conflicts and you can't even count on the people you're trying to protect. I mean — where are they? I don't see them here with you pounding on my desk.

CRUZ: The only thing I'm protecting is my work!

JORGE: All right — let's be frank. We cannot give you water because there's no water left. However — if Lerma wanted to he could send a little your way — even though he'd have to take it away from some other poor devil.

CRUZ: It could be done?

JORGE: It's risky but it's been done before. I can vouch for it. You have to agree to his price, though.

CRUZ: How much do you think he'd charge?

JORGE: That's the problem. The old guy is very greedy. I don't know if you folks would agree to . . .

CRUZ: What else can we do? Right now, the most important thing is to save the cotton.

JORGE: Let me talk to him. But don't say a word to anyone, you hear? I'll tell you later what he said.

CRUZ: *(With difficulty.)* All right then. I'll see you later, then. *(He exits.)*
(Jorge's assistant enters. Jorge says to him, smiling.)

JORGE: I pulled it off!

ASSISTANT: They're going to do it?

JORGE: Always works. Little by little I pull them in, until I've got 'em by the balls!

ASSISTANT: Gee boss, I want to grow up to be just like you!

JORGE: That'll be a bitch!

(Lights out.)

(In the countryside. Cruz looks at some plants. We start to see him losing some enthusiasm.)

CRUZ: Infestation is pretty heavy. *(To Juancho.)* You've got to apply more insecticide today.

JUANCHO: *(Surprised.)* More?!

CRUZ: You already applied some? How much?

JUANCHO: Exactly what you told me.

CRUZ: So why the hell are there so many bugs? Did everyone else already apply insecticide too?

JUANCHO: Yeah and the same things are happening to them.

(Cruz is thinking things over.)

CRUZ: We've got to fumigate all over again. This time, double the insecticide per liter of water and loan me one of your cans. I'm sending it to be analyzed. And while you're at it give me a little of the fertilizer, cause I'm not real pleased with the size of the plants either. *(He exits. Darkness.)*

(In the cantina some men are arguing.)

CUQUILLO: We've got to sell the cotton ourselves!

NAZARIO: And break the agreement we have with the government?

PILO: I don't think they'll let us.

CUQUILLO: We're not going to ask their permission!

NAZARIO: It's just that we're already committed. They even fixed a price.

CHON: Yeah sure — before we knew they were going to devalue the peso!

BONI: We could sell it for a better price right now!

PILO: How can we do that? We owe the bank so much.

GUERA: We could pay them directly.

NAZARIO: We've really got to think this one over. There'll be reprisals.

PILO: We don't even know who to sell it to Engineer Cruz says . . .

CUQUILLO: What does Cruz have to do with it. This is our problem and we got to solve it! *(David enters, frightened.)*

DAVID: Here comes Engineer Cruz!

CUQUILLO: So?

DAVID: He's drunk!

NAZARIO: Strange. I've never seen him drunk before.

CUQUILLO: It's about time he started acting like a man!

GUERA: You and your ideas about manhood! You need more guts to do what he's been doing than to be mouthing off like you.

(Along the road comes Cruz — totally inebriated.)

CRUZ: *(Singing off key.)* It was all adulterated

Very very adulterated

Everything was adulterated

The stupid insecticide was adulterated

The fertilizer was adulterated

This town is adulterated . . .

(He comes across an old man.)

And what are you? A ghost! Cross! . . . Cross! . . . *(Holds up his fingers in sign of the cross.)* OOPS! Cross — Cruz, Cruz — that's me! That's me. *(The old man looks at him astonished.)*

Do I know you from somewhere? Have we fought before? *(The old man steps back.)* No? Then you're not from here — cuz here . . . I've fought with everyone! Do you wanna fight? *(The old man flees.)* Don't worry — lately I've been losing every fight!

(Cruz arrives at the cantina and enters. The men look at him perplexed and silently.)

CRUZ: Ladies and gentlemen — Tenochtlen's Public Enemy Number One has arrived! Give me a bottle, Guera . . . of whatever. *(To the others.)* I've just come from Police headquarters. I was only there a little while . . . I went to file a complaint against the distributor because the insecticide was adulterated. Hey, what happened to my bottle? *(He drinks.)* And you can all rejoice! They're gonna fire the guy in charge of insecticide . . . but in his place they're gonna put his twin brother? Hey — who's fucking with my bottle?

Oh here's good ole Cuquillo! Shall we beat the crap out of each other? *(Cuquillo watches him.)* Well — just seeing the fear on your face makes me happy . . . Ah and I've got other news. This is better yet. *(He takes a wrinkled piece of paper out of his pocket. He reads.)* Terminating your contract, we hereby notify you that as of this date your services are no longer required by the Cooperative Extension. This means, to the joy of each and every person present . . . and even those not present, I am leaving! Soooooo that's why I came here to say good-bye to all my friends in Tenochtlen and to thank you for your spontaneous support, your kind cooperation and for all the comradeship you've shown me. *(He can't continue because of all the emotion that rises up in him. He takes refuge in a drink.)*

NAZARIO: Mister Engineer, Benito wants to talk to you tomorrow morning.

CRUZ: Tomorrow is another day . . . Guera! Get me a big piece of ice. I'm going to write down my new address. *(He starts to fall but Pilo holds him up. However, Cruz pushes him away.)*
Let me go! *(Wounded.)*
One thing I want to make very clear: I didn't come here, like the others, just to fuck you over. I didn't do that. You'll do well with the cotton — even after all the fuckups, the betrayals, the shit that was done to us — with all of that — you'll still earn as much as you would have by planting corn and beans like you always do. So, all your hate and your anger against me didn't cost a thing! *(Juancho enters upset.)*

JUANCHO: They just raised the price of beans and corn! It's almost doubled! *(Everyone is upset now.)*

GUERA: Jesus! There'll be hunger again in Tenochtlen. *(Silence.)*

CRUZ: Ohhh Don Maximo . . . you bastard! *(He throws his bottle against the wall and exits. Lights out.)*
(The outside of Maximo's house. Cruz knocks uselessly on the door. No one answers. He's still under the effects of alcohol.)

CRUZ: Maximo! . . . Maximo! . . . Open up! I want to congratulate you on your ingenuity. You really know how to do things. You're very smart, shrewd. You know how to milk every last drop out of all us retards here. Open up! Come on! Don't be afraid. Open! *(He despairs.)* Open mother fucker or I'll break every window in your house. Okay, I warned you. You asked for it.
(He throws one stone and breaks the glass. He laughs. He breaks another one. He is having fun. He gathers a bunch of stones ready to throw more when the door opens. Cruz goes to enter but two men with clubs come out and beat him until he's unconscious. They exit. He lies there among the stones he gathered and the dust of the road. Lights out.)
(A little later we see a shadow in the darkness. It is Manuela.)

MANUELA: Cruz! Cruz! *(She finds him.)* Cruz — Oh my God — Look what they did to you! *(She tries to rouse him.)*

CRUZ: Hey . . . what? What? *(With great effort he gets up and tries to walk. He is badly hurt.)*
Ay, Jesus, I think they've left me paralyzed . . . *(They walk towards the camp. Manuela can hardly hold him up.)*

MANUELA: You shouldn't provoke him!

CRUZ: *(Semiconscious.)* Who? Ouch! *(They exit.)*

THE SONG OF TWO EMOTIONS

Two emotions have awakened
Two fundamental emotions.
One is the anger of betrayal
The other the love of the faithful.

Today a man rebels against his fate
The fate he was born with and marked.
Those who sow lies in this country
Reap crops harvested in infamy.

I give you my life full of anger
Give me your warmth and your truth.
I give you my fists full of hatred
Show me the road that is fated.

Words and music by Gabino Palomares

BALLADEER: *(Recites.)* They walked for over an hour, guided by the rising moon that burned — perhaps in pity, perhaps to give some warmth to these two wandering souls.

(On the road — they are slowly making their way to the camp.)

CRUZ: I feel all twisted and swollen. I must look like that hunchback Quasimodo.

MANUELA: You'll feel better soon, you'll see. I'm going to heal you.

CRUZ: Do you know that this is the first time someone's been nice to me since I got to Tenochtlen? *(They've arrived. They open the door to Cruz's house and enter. The girl helps Cruz lie down and removes his clothes. She fills the wash basin with water and prepares something medicinal. Then she returns to the bed and begins to bathe his wounds. The contact with water makes Cruz cry out in pain.)*

MANUELA: Does that hurt a lot?

CRUZ: Yes, yes!

MANUELA: Well, bite the pillow, because now it's going to hurt you worse! *(She grabs a bottle of mezcal and empties it over the wounds. Cruz groans with the pillow in his mouth.)*

MANUELA: *(Sweetly.)* It's over. It's all over.

CRUZ: So that's why you came to get me . . . so you could torture me, right?

MANUELA: I won't hurt you anymore. I'm done. I'm going to bring you some pills for the pain. *(Cruz holds her arm to stop her.)*

CRUZ: No, don't go!

MANUELA: It's only to get . . .

CRUZ: It does me good to have you here — better than any pill. *(Manuela sits down on the side of the bed.)* Why have you waited so long to get near me?

MANUELA: Everything in this town moves very slowly. *(She smiles.)*

CRUZ: *(He tries to reach out to her but it hurts him.)* Ouch!

MANUELA: Try not to move.

CRUZ: They got me good. This is what I get for trying to be a saviour. I remember, when I was little, I liked this little sign that my father had over his desk. It said, "Help me Lord, not to get mixed up in what's none of my business." But I've been sticking my nose into other people's business for twenty five years now. *(Laughs.)*

MANUELA: *(Serious.)* But we are your business. *(Cruz takes her hand and Manuela is nervous.)*

MANUELA: Now, I have to go. It's late.

CRUZ: Wait. Manuela. Don't go. Please.

(Gently, Manuela moves toward the door.)

CRUZ: Manuela really, I'm so alone.

(Manuela turns and looks at him for a long moment. In her eyes a strange mixture of desire and compassion. Then she makes a decision and without hesitating she goes to the door and turns out the light. She goes back to the bed and takes off her clothing and lies down next to him.)

LOVE SONG (Cancion de Amor)
Here, where there seems to be no time for illusions
Here, where they murder your dignity and grace
Here, where the simplest ones live in pain
Here, here is home and love's terrain.

Now imprisoned spring will burst forth and fly
Now ice cracks and winter will melt and die
Now night is potent and reclaims its heat
Now, our bodies crave love's song so sweet.

Come to me, I want to climb your mountain of kisses
Come to me, So we can glimpse the future of our wishes

Come, so together we can reach the highest truth
And then return to find our happiness is good.

(The next morning. Manuela is preparing coffee and Cruz watches her. They both seem very happy.)

CRUZ: You're so pretty, Manuela.

MANUELA: You too.

CRUZ: When did you start to like me?

MANUELA: Since that afternoon when you were wandering around lost . . .

CRUZ: So why did you wait so long?

MANUELA: I thought you were full of yourself — treating us all so casually like we were little children.

CRUZ: You mean that was it?

MANUELA: We're not used to that. We're more formal. So in the beginning everyone thought you were a jerk. *(Smiles.)* That's why you and Benito didn't get along.

CRUZ: Just because I was casual?

MANUELA: Overfamiliar right away and you didn't even know us.

CRUZ: I was that bad?

MANUELA: Not bad exactly, because it's just your way, because you act familiar with everyone. The other engineers were different. They'd be familiar, overfamiliar with us because they think we're inferior. They look down on us.

CRUZ: You're too sensitive!

MANUELA: No. It's true.

CRUZ: How can you tell?

MANUELA: It's simple. When they're with the rich they change completely. Uy! They're bowing and scraping, they're so respectful; believe me, not one of them was casual with Don Maximo — but with my father who is more respectable by far than that man, they'd slap him on the back and treat him like a child. Why do you think that is? Could it be that the only thing they respect is money?

CRUZ: Who knew? I can't believe how much I have to learn here.

MANUELA: You were different. When you met Don Maximo — Juancho saw you treated him like any other guy — just like you treated us.

CRUZ: That's not true. I never, never treated Don Maximo the way I treat you. *(He pulls her down on top of him and they kiss and wrestle affectionately. Then serious.)* Manuela would you like to live in the city?

MANUELA: Oh, you mean where I'd be such a success?

CRUZ: *(Kissing her.)* You do hold grudge!

MANUELA: But no. Not in the city. There you're one of many. Here the people are good, they look out for you.

CRUZ: Manuela, you know I'll come back for you, don't you?

MANUELA: You're leaving?

CRUZ: I have to! I have to find work. It's for the better. Now I'll never work with Don Maximo and his people, and it seems that with you folks I just came to wipe you out completely.

MANUELA: *(Softly.)* My father doesn't want you to go . . . I don't either.

CRUZ: Now you tell me! But if I stayed who would support me?

MANUELA: We would.

CRUZ: You and Benito . . . well that would be just fine but . . .

MANUELA: No all of us, the whole town.

CRUZ: What?

MANUELA: Yes, the whole town wants you to stay and give us technical assistance, you are an agricultural engineer aren't you?

CRUZ: Even Cuquillo?

MANUELA: Even Cuquillo. That's why my father wants you to go see him. He already talked to all our neighbors and they all agreed to contribute and pay your salary.

CRUZ: *(Very moved.)* Really? After everything I've put them through?

MANUELA: Yes. Everyone knows now you did it all in good faith and they love you, Cruz. Now they know you're a truly good man and they really care for you. *(Cruz goes under the covers. Manuela is frightened.)* Cruz! What's the matter? Are you sick? *(She struggles to uncover him and finally does.)* What's wrong?

CRUZ: Nothing. *(He can barely speak.)* I . . . I'm fine. It's just . . . I'm very emotional. I was ashamed for you to see me cry. *(Lights out.)*
(The Love Song is repeated. Lights out.)
(A meeting at Benito's house.)

BENITO: *(To Cruz.)* Well, as you can see, we can't offer you much — and less this year when we're really broke — but if you stick with us a little the next crop will be . . .

CRUZ: Don't worry. Benito, I have some savings — So if you can see your way to helping me with room and board, I'm in. *(General rejoicing.)*
What's important now is what we're going to do, and I have three very concrete proposals for you.

JUANCHO: Whatever you say, Cruz!

CRUZ: First — you need to be more formal with me, you're way too familiar.

(*He laughs.*) No. Not really (*Everyone else laughs when they get the joke.*) My first thought has to do with what we can plant after the cotton — so we can recover some of our losses. It has to be an emergency crop with a short cheap growing cycle, since the cotton crop is already mortgaged to the bank and once we pay them off we'll have almost nothing to go on with.

CUQUILLO: Hey, Cruz!

CRUZ: What's up, Cuquillo?

CUQUILLO: Do we have to pay them?

CRUZ: I don't understand.

CUQUILLO: Well, I'm only saying this, but why are we always the ones to put up with their shit?

CRUZ: What do you mean?

CUQUILLO: Why not "tit for tat" you know, do unto others as they have done unto you? (*The others laugh.*) Let's give them some of their own medicine.

CRUZ: (*Serious.*) It's not out of the question. After all, it's the bank's fault that our production was so low and the debt so high. But I don't see how we can not pay them — if the bank itself is doing the harvesting.

JUANCHO: Yes, but not for a week . . . that's when the pickers come from La Laguna I found out.

BONI: (*Maliciously.*) So, we could beat them to it.

PILO: At night — when no one sees us.

> (*Here, everyone begins to take up a sack and goes to the field without interrupting the following dialogues.*)

NAZARIO: We could go through the canyon to the valley, so we won't bump into the rural police.

BENITO: If we push hard we could pick more than half the cotton in four nights.

GUERA: Yeah, let the bank and those other thieves collect from what's left over.

> (*Now everyone is picking cotton in the field.*)

BALLADEER: (*Recites.*) Wait till you see their faces

When the bank sees all this

When they find the cotton gone

By an act of God

Their profits turned to piss.

> (*They all laugh.*)

CRUZ: (*Picking.*) Don't pick the cotton plants so evenly. If you pick a little here and there, it won't be noticed as much.

PILO: And what are we going to say when they ask for their cotton?

CHON: Well, that the insecticide they gave us didn't do shit. The bugs ate it up. *(They laugh.)*

BONI: We even got buckets of it we can show 'em.

CRUZ: What isn't clear to me is how we're going to manage to sell the cotton?

BENITO: Don Nazario has already spoken to the people at the mill in La Laguna. For a small commission, they'll sell our cotton for us, mixed in with theirs.

MANUELA: The truck's here!

BENITO: Start loading the sacks. *(The truck goes, comes out loaded, and the men sit down to wait for the next trip. They talk among themselves.)*

PILO: One thing's for sure. After this, we can't dream of asking for credit again.

GUERA: Or water for irrigation

MANUELA: Why not? It's not even theirs.

CUQUILLO: Of course! If they won't give us water, we'll tear down their canals and then let's see what they'll do.

BONI: They'd shoot us.

CUQUILLO: Then we'd shoot them.

CRUZ: No. No we can't let this deteriorate into violence. We're the ones who would lose.

CUQUILLO: So what — we're gonna let them walk all over us?

CRUZ: No, we have to defend ourselves in another way.

CUQUILLO: How?

CRUZ: I can't say exactly. But we have a Constitution, laws that protect us.

GUERA: Well yeah — but they're the ones in charge of the laws.

CRUZ: If we stay united we can pressure them into applying the laws correctly.

CUQUILLO: *(Skeptically.)* Right!

NAZARIO: What do you think about this, Don Benito?

BENITO: *(Scratching his head.)* Well, Benito agrees with the engineer when he says we should try to avoid an armed conflict with these people. We're not prepared. Blood would flow — and uselessly and that's not what we want, or is it? *(Murmurs of "no," etc.)* But, we got to be very alert. This is the first time they're on the losing side and they are not going to like it and they're not going to take this sitting down. We got to think this over — how will they take their revenge? Benito doesn't know yet. Maybe they'll take something out of our next crop or pressure us with the matter of land ownership . . . they got so many ways to get at us . . . and us, we got very little to hold over them. Only our hands and this cotton we're taking. And I ask you what are we gonna do when we sell it? Buy alcohol so we can act like animals. Buy a TV and then go beg these guys for credit again? *(The people disapprove.)* Or before anything else, do we buy the grain we need to eat and to plant?

JUANCHO: That's exactly what we need to do! *(General support.)*

BENITO: We can buy corn for the rest of the year and some animals that can get us through bad times. Then whatever else happens we won't go hungry. As long as we're one year ahead — they can't touch us. We won't starve.

BONI: The truck's back!

(They load the truck and then stand together to listen to Cruz.)

CRUZ: Ah yes — the second thought I wanted to present to you — is that you help me with technical assistance. Now that we've worked together a bit, I can see that I have more to learn from you than you from me. *(Laughter.)* Maybe my only advantage is that when we get hit out of nowhere by a plague that neither of us knows how to combat, I know where to go, what to ask, and who to talk to, to get the best information. That's the only thing I can really teach you. So if one day I have to leave, you'll know how to do this yourselves. The rest we'll learn together and together we'll undertake *(The men begin to disperse.)* some measures that will make things come out better next time. For example, we have to do a study of the soils here to see which crops would be easiest to grow in this region.

CHON: We have the soil samples ready — just like you told us.

CRUZ: Then we need to gather some statistics so we can evaluate whatever we undertake.

NAZARIO: *(With a package.)* We've already filled out the forms you gave us, Engi — See if we did them right.

CRUZ: And it is indispensable that we organize an literacy campaign immediately in Tenochtlen so that there's not one of you who can't read and write. Those of us who already know how — will teach the rest of you!

(Some of the peasants sit around Manuela.)

MANUELA: A for animal . . . for action . . . for advise . . . for agitator.

CRUZ: When we can all read and write — it won't be so easy to take advantage of us!

MANUELA: B for burro, for bank, bandit, bastards.

CRUZ: And since we're all interested in saving this land where we were born.

MANUELA: R . . .

ALL: For revolution!

(Cruz moves away and the people gather around him.)

CRUZ: My last proposal is the following: as I said before I don't need money right now, but by next harvest time, yes, I'm going to want you guys to make an effort to give me a salary. I want to have enough so I can buy a few animals, a little house and above all enough to support Manuela who I want to marry me.

(Manuela enters resplendent in a bridal gown.)

GUERA: Long live the Bride and Groom!

(Rapidly they put a black suit jacket on Cruz who embraces her. Various neighbors enter bringing a table that is already decorated. The Balladeer arrives dressed as a Mariachi and a party begins. Everyone is having a good time and it lasts for a while until the sudden entrance of Quirino and two deputies armed with rifles.)

QUIRINO: Nobody moves and no one's hurt! *(Everyone remains stupefied.)*

BENITO: *(Confronting them.)* What right do you have to come into this house!

QUIRINO: You're the one we're looking for! You and Lopez! Grab them!

(Cruz pushes the deputy who's coming for him and goes up to Quirino.)

CRUZ: One moment here. What are we accused of ?

QUIRINO: You know what you're accused of.

CRUZ: Where's our arrest order. You can't arrest anyone without a judicial order!

QUIRINO: If you resist, things will go worse for you. The house is surrounded.

CRUZ: This is called breaking and entering — and it's a crime. Get out of here right now!

(The deputy who was pushed comes up behind Cruz and hits him with the butt of the rifle. Cruz falls to the ground.)

MANUELA: Cruz!

(Cuquillo jumps on the deputy and hits him. The deputy falls. The other deputy hits Cuquillo with his rifle and then points it at his chest. The other deputy gets up and also points his rifle at Cuquillo.)

CUQUILLO: Very macho — eh — you and your rifles!

QUIRINO: The next one who moves, shoot him!

GUERA: But why are you arresting them?

QUIRINO: Chief's orders.

BENITO: Cruz is right. You can't just force your way into a house and beat people up — not by no one's orders!

QUIRINO: You must obey authority!

(The other farmers have armed themselves with sticks and bottles and little by little they go towards the door and block it.)

QUIRINO: *(To the deputies.)* Get 'em outta the way!

JUANCHO: *(Breaks a bottle and uses it as a weapon.)* No. Quirino, the only ones leaving this place are you and your men.

QUIRINO: Yeah? We'll see who's getting out of here or not. Rifles up!

CUQUILLO: You may kill a few of us, but you'll die too.

QUIRINO: Get away from that door! *(No one moves.)* Deputies, when I give the order — fire! Ready . . . aim . . .

CRUZ: Wait . . . Wait . . . Let us go. Juancho, there's no need to provoke a massacre. *(To Quirino.)* Come on. We'll go with you.

MANUELA: No Cruz! *(She embraces him.)*

CRUZ: Don't worry, they have nothing to accuse us of. *(He separates her from him.)* We'll be back in an hour.

QUIRINO: Let's go. Come on! *(They begin to leave.)*

BENITO: *(To Manuela.)* All the same. Start getting everyone together in case they hold us too long!

(They exit.)

MANUELA: Juancho, go with them. Don't let them out of your sight! Chon, go call everyone together. *(She removes her bridal gown.)*

DAVID: *(Coming out of the house.)* Here's your old man's rifle, Manuela!

MANUELA: *(Takes it and turns to the others.)* And the rest of you, aren't you going to get your guns?

PILO: *(Frightened.)* Our guns? What for?

MANUELA: What do you mean, what for? — to go rescue Cruz and my father.

BONI: Shouldn't we first wait to see what happens?

MANUELA: Wait for what? *(Shouting.)* Wait for what?

GUERA: *(Trying to calm her down.)* Take it easy, Manuela — you're very upset and this is no way to make a decision. Nothing's going to happen to them.

CUQUILLO: I agree with Manuela — we can't wait until something happens to them!

BONI: You heard Cruz. They can't do anything to them. There's nothing to fear.

MANUELA: He said that so they wouldn't fire on all of you.

NAZARIO: No Manuela, Cruz has always been against violence.

CUQUILLO: But who's violent? Them or us?

BALLADEER: *(To the audience.)* And now, here's the scene you saw at the top of the play.

MANUELA: If you're with me — follow me now!

NAZARIO: Wait, Manuela. We're outmanned. Don't be so impulsive. There's too many.

CUQUILLO: Shit, who's counting! My men are with you, Manuela. We've had enough! *(His men call out their support.)*

BONI: But we're not even organized!

PILO: We don't even know what to do! *(Murmurs of doubt.)*

MANUELA: We'll surround city hall and demand their return. How much organization do we need for that?!

NAZARIO: At least we should know who and how . . . outline a plan.

CUQUILLO: Let's go, Manuela. Forget these shit faced cowards . . .

NAZARIO: Watch who you're calling coward . . . you . . .

I ain't afraid of no one. What I'm worried about is what if we go marching over there armed and shit and they take it as a provocation. Then yeah, they'll really take it out on Cruz and Benito.

MANUELA: *(In doubt.)* Oh God. Now I don't know what to do.

(The door opens and Juancho enters wounded. Guera sees him and runs over to him.)

GUERA: Juancho! My God! What happened to you?

JUANCHO: They killed them, Manuela. They killed them!

MANUELA: *(Paralyzed, can almost not get the words out.)* Wha . . . ?

JUANCHO: The deputies began to walk slowly and trailed behind Cruz and your father. Then they shot them in the back. *(He almost can't talk.)* I think so they could say later that they tried to escape. *(Dies.)*

GUERA: JUANCHO!

(Manuela lets out a moan and raises her rifle as if she wants to shoot in the air. In that moment the scene freezes. The Balladeer addresses the audience again.)

BALLADEER: This is where the story of the Agronomist finds itself at this moment . . . Now it's up to you to give it an ending.

(The actors break out of their freeze and go to the front of the stage. They're not acting now.)

BALLADEER: So we ask for some suggestions on how, in your opinion, this play should end. We'll take a few suggestions and discuss them and then, finally you'll vote for the ending you'd like us to act out for you. Okay? (If there aren't anymore questions, doubts, etc.) Let's see . . . you . . . what do you think?

(And as the Balladeer stated, various opinions will be heard. The most interesting will be filled in, discussed and voted on and then the ending will be added as suggested by the audience.)

(It would also be valuable to bring along some of the written endings proposed by different audiences. It's possible that with time this play will find its proper ending.)

END OF PLAY

Cancion de Amor

El Corrido de Tenochtlen

El Corrido de Tenochtlen
page 2

El Corrido de Tenochtlen
page 3

THE UNWRITTEN LAW
A Nightmare In Two Acts

On March 4, 1987, the president of Mexico's Institutional Revolutionary Party (PRI) officially announced to the public and media the existence of an "unwritten law" which ruled the destiny of our country.

We knew this law existed, we had felt it in our everyday lives, but its public acknowledgment still caused surprise in this country of surprises.

The story of H is a tribute by this author to this unwritten law.

Felipe Santander

IN REGARD TO MY WORK

Many years ago, Miranda, my first wife — a native of Plymouth, UK, became friendly with a group of foreign women married to Mexican men. This group of young women called themselves "Las Desperadas" (The Desperate Women) and met once a week at a cafe to vent against our machismo, irresponsibility, unfair treatment, economic insolvency and more — being able, (in these meetings) to experience a seven-day group catharsis of sorts. I first met H outside the cafe, where we husbands were waiting for our respective wives. We began a friendship that lasted several years. Later H began working for the Department of Cinematography, and I got involved in the Government Extension Program. We lost touch. When H found himself involved in a big scandal and was sent to prison, I was running around the Mexican countryside. But even then — from afar — I followed his trial very closely.

My version of H's story is full of alterations and anachronisms like all my work (I am a playwright, not an historian). To begin with, I had H meet up with some of the more conspicuous prisoners of the day — a secretary of state, the president of a political party, drug traffickers and so on. I am not sure if H actually did meet these people, or if it was even possible that he might have, but that is not important. What's essential is the lesson H receives once he is in prison — if not exactly from those people then from people very much like them. The biggest change I made in the story, however, is the ending. In reality, H is still alive. My ending is more or less symbolic.

In general terms, the first scene of the play, the suffering in prison, and the wanderings through the streets in the second act can be taken as pure Mexican folklore of the 80's. The central characters are well-known in Mexican society — so that to try and separate what is real and what is fiction would be quite difficult. It's easier to point out which details don't belong to H. For example, the cardboard box is based on something that actually happened to me when I was with the Government Extension Program. The scene with the Traffic Cop is only an obsessive fantasy of mine. The sequence with Brat is based on a party I was invited to, and the nurse in the story was a girlfriend of mine. I incorporated these incidents into H's story — but I tried to keep all the essential elements of his story intact.

TO END WITH AN ANECDOTE . . .

I was aware of how difficult it would be to get a production of *The Unwritten Law* in Mexico. To quote an often used official phrase which is both eloquent and subtle: "Why the hell should we give him money so he can criticize us?" . . . which in turn implies, "Why should we lend him one of our theaters" or "Why give him permission and license to do something we don't like," and even, "Why should we let him keep on living in Mexico anyway?" For the country's bosses — even living is a concession they can give. I did, however, find one possible solution . . .

The Writers' Union (SOGEM) funded an annual play contest with six very respectable judges. The first prize was a production of the winning play. None of the best Mexican playwrights entered this contest — to have their play debut in a bad theater, with a mediocre cast and lousy publicity? No thanks! This contest was really for new playwrights who were desperate to have their work brought to the public no matter what! I immediately submitted my play — since I was actually in the same situation as they were. The important thing for me was to get this play produced by SOGEM, which would then give me the right to produce it later in another venue and without the pressure of competing with other, better, writers.

Finally the contest took place and the results were made known very tersely. Virgilio Rivera, a good young author, was the winner. But no other information was given out. I was curious. I wanted at least to know how I had placed in the contest. I went to a lover of mine who happened to work at SOGEM, who after a bit of begging told me that I had been in second place, two points below Virgilio. She also told me that one of the judges didn't want to grade my piece. Intrigued, I asked to see the files. I found mine with a note by one of the deacons of the critics that said: "This is by far the best work here, but it's very dangerous and I don't dare grade it. You do what you want to with it." And "poof" with his refusal, ten points were taken off my score. (The judges' grades usually fluctuated between five and ten — and never less than five in the entire history of the contest. Those five points would have guaranteed me first place.) So, pissed off, I went to SOGEM and threatened them with a scandal. Secretary Usain told me that nothing could be done. . . .

(It wasn't me
It was him
Hit him, hit him
On the chin)

But he also told me that, as *The Unwritten Law* had won second place, it would be produced anyway, and in a better theater, in a better production with better publicity and with actors of my choosing blah, blah, blah. It never happened. Secretary Usain preferred to die (he did) before he premiered my play — which like H — is still wandering around out there on the city streets.

CHARACTERS

H
His Wife
The Chief
His Subordinate
Co-op Farmers
Gangbanger
Nightclub Performer
Actor
Guard
Little Old Lady
Torturer
Professor
H's Father-in-Law (Papa)
Lawyer
H's Mother
Big Shot
Capo
Exotic Dancer
Driver
Traffic Cop
Neighbor Woman
Ice Cream Man
Brat
Christ
Secretary
Faith
Nurse
The Señora (H's Boss)
Also: Guards, common prisoners, prisoner's visitors, H's wife's family, Capo's men, street people, drug people, artists and guests at Brat's blowout party, office employees, the Señora's servants.

The actors may double in many parts and the cast can be filled out with dummies or puppets.

ACT ONE
SCENE ONE: A Difficult Day

In H's house in Satellite City.
It is midnight. A ray of light slides through the window and across the floor onto the bed until it illuminates H's face. He can't sleep and is lying there staring fixedly at the wall. His wife is asleep next to him, snoring quietly. Suddenly there's a break in her rhythm. She turns restlessly. She sits up and without totally waking, she goes to the bathroom. H doesn't seem to notice. Through the door we hear his wife urinate, flush the toilet, turn the water on and then the light being turned off. His wife returns to bed and notices her husband.

WIFE: Oh! . . . oh . . .
  (H seems hypnotized. His wife passes her hand in front of his eyes. He murmurs.)
H: It didn't ring.
WIFE: Huh?
H: It never rang.
WIFE: Tsk.
H: It didn't ring once . . . all day!
  (Pause.)
WIFE: *(Hesitantly.)* What . . . didn't ring?
H: The telephone! *(Desperate.)* It never rang the whole day!
WIFE: Strange. But Carmen called me on it yesterday!
H: My phone. My office phone!
WIFE: Oh, I see . . . And?
H: All day, waiting, lighting each cigarette with the next until I had such a coughing fit the whole office was alarmed . . .
WIFE: You shouldn't smoke so much.
H: And the phone never rang.
WIFE: Maybe it was broken.
H: *(Yelling.)* No! It was fine! I checked. It just didn't ring.
  (Pause.)
WIFE: And . . . it was very important that it did ring?
H: Important? The telephone is vital! It's the heart, the energy, the dynamic of the whole office. Everything depends on the phone — everything! Appointments, agreements, contracts, contacts, rejections, recommendations . . . and all of a sudden "poof."

WIFE: Poof?

H: Yes — poof, poof, poof!

(He covers his face with his hands in agony.)

WIFE: Don't be upset. Shall I make you some tea? . . . a drink?

H: No thank you.

WIFE: Let's have a drink to relax . . . and then watch . . . our film?

H: *(Briskly.)* Please! I've been awake for hours trying to find a reason, something, anything that will help me understand why!

WIFE: You worry too much. Ever since they made you director of that cinematography thing.

H: Institute! Only the most important job of my life!

WIFE: Well yes, but look what it's done to you! You stay up all night agonizing over everything. You've only been there a month and you've been sick to your stomach every day — and all because of some statements the Señora made to the press.

H: Those statements might cost me my job!

WIFE: I've read them over and over and I can't find anything that would apply to you!

H: You have to read between the lines: when the Señora complained that even her closest aides were turning against her, it's obvious she was referring to that interview I gave where I said "We'll have to try to adjust to a budget that's not quite as roomy as it has been in years past." And that stupid reporter published that we were planning to gut the country's film industry!

WIFE: Hey, maybe that problem with the phone did have to do with . . . .

H: No. It's more recent than that.

WIFE: *(Worried.)* You gave another interview?

H: You can't get out of them. But I'm more cautious now, I don't compromise myself. The only thing I said in the last one was that the cultural development of a country couldn't depend on politics based on seances and astrological signs.

WIFE: Why did you say that?

H: Come on — that's indisputable — it can't offend anyone. The only kind of opinions I give nowadays are completely inoffensive. No, where I feel vulnerable is in my work.

WIFE: But you work so hard!

H: Well sure, but it's hard to do what you're supposed to when your boss improvises and contradicts herself all the time.

WIFE: You mean the Señora?

H: *(Nods.)* When she says right to your face that "I've been asking you to attend to this since last week" and you fall all over yourself apologizing for your negligence when she never mentioned it in the first place.

WIFE: Forget about it and let's go to sleep.

H: You can sleep if you want to! I'm a little upset.

WIFE: *(Lively.)* Really? Maybe there's something I can do for you.

(She embraces him. H doesn't know what to do. He doesn't feel romantic but he also doesn't want to hurt her feelings. He plays around with her a little then he kisses her, tucks her in and he turns on his side away from her. But she isn't satisfied with this arrangement and renews her advances.)

WIFE: *(Laughing like a naughty child.)* I can't sleep either!

H: Take a pill.

WIFE: It's been more than a week since we've seen . . . our film.

H: *(Alarmed.)* That long?

WIFE: Nine days exactly. Shall I turn it on, hmmmm?

H: But I have to work tomorrow.

WIFE: You're not tired and neither am I. Don't be like that . . .

H: I'm very anxious.

WIFE: Trust me, this will calm you down, you'll see.

H: Okay.

(The wife jumps out of bed and turns on the video.)

WIFE: You're in charge of the drinks.

(She goes into the bathroom. H takes out a bottle of cognac and some glasses. He gives himself a shot first to fortify himself. In the bathroom we hear the wife sprucing up. She comes out in sexy underwear.)

WIFE: *(Sensually.)* My drink.

(H gives it to her. She sips it. They refill their glasses and sit down to watch a video that lights up their faces. It's a pornographic film where we only hear the dialogue in some foreign language, music and some sounds. Soon they begin to respond. H sweats and licks his lips, the woman gives little cries and moans. Then they put aside their glasses and drink right from the bottle. The woman begins to lose control.)

WIFE: Ay . . . Oh my God . . . no . . . no. Did you see that? Ay . . . you won't do that to me will you? Ay no . . . what beasts, what savages!

(Finally she climbs on top of H and seduces him.)

(A little later they are deeply asleep. The TV is still on.)

(All of a sudden the bedroom lights go on and two tall and muscular men dressed like government agents enter. They search the room with total disregard for the sleeping couple.)

CHIEF: *(He sees H.)* Is this the man?

(The subordinate takes out a photo and compares it to H.)

SUBORDINATE: Yeah. That's him.

CHIEF: Stay there next to him in case he wakes up.

(He goes to the window, then looks at the mess on the floor.)

SUBORDINATE: *(Maliciously.)* They won't wake up. It looks like they really tied one on.

CHIEF: What's that noise?

SUBORDINATE: They left the TV on.

CHIEF: Turn it off.

(The subordinate goes to turn it off but the program attracts his attention.)

SUBORDINATE: Hey Chief — you should see what an interesting plot this has.

CHIEF: I can't hear you. Turn it off.

(The subordinate lowers the volume but keeps watching the TV.)

SUBORDINATE: I turned down the sound.

CHIEF: Where the hell is our back-up! He must have gone to a gas station in Siberia, for Christsakes. *(He sees the sub's face.)* And you — what's your problem — what you making faces for?

SUBORDINATE: Just come over and take a look.

(The Chief walks up to the TV and peers at it. He's surprised.)

CHIEF: What the fuck . . . So that's what these folks were watching? *(He sits on the bed.)* Jesus! That cannon can't be real, or is it? Shit, he's gonna split her in two!

(They are both entranced by the TV. Turning in bed, the wife exposes one of her legs and the Chief starts getting ideas.)

CHIEF: Make sure this guy doesn't get up.

(He uncovers the woman who is sleeping on her stomach and adjusts her; the Chief catches the sub watching his every move and gets mad.)

CHIEF: Fuck you — watch the TV . . . and turn out the light.

(The sub obeys. The Chief gets on top of the woman who is unconscious, after three moans that sound more like snorts, the Chief finishes and gets up. The sub points to himself.)

SUBORDINATE: Now me, Chief? Okay?

CHIEF: No. It's late.

SUBORDINATE: A quickie . . .

CHIEF: I said no! Control yourself. Can't you see we're on duty? Better, go wake up that guy.

(The sub obeys reluctantly. he turns on the lamp on the n ight table and sits on the bed and slaps H twice. H is startled awake. The sub covers H's mouth

with his fat hand. Still hazy from the alcohol and surprise, H doesn't react except for opening his eyes wide and looking from one man to the other.)
(All of a sudden he thinks about his wife and turns to her.)

CHIEF: Shhhhh. She's sleeping. Why disturb her?

(H makes them understand how uncomfortable he is with the hairy paw over his mouth. The Chief signals the subordinate to let H loose.)

H: *(Very nervous.)* Can I smoke?

(The Chief throws him some cigarettes.)

CHIEF: You can do whatever the hell you want — just don't scream and don't cause a ruckus.

(H smokes. He considers the situation without knowing what to do. These men look too ferocious for him to attempt any heroic gesture. Besides which, they're probably armed. However, he's worried about his wife. The gorilla in front of the TV seems capable of almost any atrocity. And moreover, he's turned on by the stupid porn film that it occurred to H and his wife to watch.)

SUBORDINATE: Look at this, Chief — now she's doing it with two guys at the same time!

CHIEF: Will ya turn that off already.

SUBORDINATE: Aw, don't be like that.

(The Chief goes to the TV and turns it off. H breathes a sign of relief. The Chief goes back to the window. Now the sub directs his attention to H and gives him a leering smile.)

SUBORDINATE: So you guys like those films? *(H doesn't know how to answer.)* Her too? Does she get all horny?

H: That woman is my wife and we're here in the privacy of our home, so whatever stimulus helps our marital relations is valid.

SUBORDINATE: I guess you guys need this filth to get it on.

H: *(Getting angry.)* And who are you to judge what pressures a man like me is under . . . how overworked I am . . . and . . . and finally — it's none of your business! Go ahead take what you want and leave us in peace!

CHIEF: *(Furious.)* What do you mean by that?!

H: I understand the situation and I'm not going to resist.

(The Chief grabs H's face in one hand and moves him like a puppet.)

CHIEF: You accusing us of being thieves? *(He shakes him.)* And what have we stolen to make you insult us like this?

H: Then . . . why are you in our house? Who are you guys?

CHIEF: You're in the hands of the law, asshole!

H: *(Astonished.)* The police?

SUBORDINATE: Doing our duty!

H: *(Uncertain.)* And . . . who are you looking for?

(The men look at each other and laugh.)

SUBORDINATE: Wellll . . . for you.

H: For me? What for?

(The men look at each other and frown.)

CHIEF: *(Confused.)* We don't know.

H: Let me see your orders of arrest.

(The men look at each other not knowing what to do. H counterattacks.)

H: So! You've broken into my home, into my very bedroom and without a judicial order you intend to take me by force?

CHIEF: By force? No. Well, unless you resist.

H: Well, I have something to say to you; you are getting yourselves into big trouble . . . BIG trouble! 'Cause in case you didn't know, this country has laws that prohibit breaking into someone's home without a judicial order, a written judicial order, and much less allows the arbitrary detention of a citizen without a penal order of arrest. So you see, I am going to ask you, in the most polite way, to get out of my house right now or . . .

(He can't finish his speech because a pair of pants falls over his head.)

CHIEF: Get dressed!

(His shirt, tie and shoes are all given to him in the same way. We hear a car's horn. The Chief goes to the window. H attempts to get his jacket but he can't because the Chief turns, takes him down with one punch and puts his knee on H's chest. The sub, taking advantage of the situation, wraps the still unconscious woman in a sheet and carries her into the bathroom.)

CHIEF: Trying to act smart?

H: My wallet's in my jacket. I was going to take it out.

CHIEF: *(Maliciously.)* Maybe you were going for your pistol, eh?

H: I don't have a pistol. I can prove it.

(The Chief goes to H's jacket and confirms that there's no weapon. He finds the wallet and gives it to H. H opens it and takes out his credentials and shows them to the Chief who is confused because he was expecting money for a bribe.)

H: This will prove that my arrest is a mistake. Look, my military service card, my driver's license — see no arrests . . . ah and the most important: a letter showing my official appointment to the post I presently occupy.

(H gives all these to the Chief who looks at them stupidly.)

CHIEF: What's all this?

H: I'm showing you proof of my high official status.

CHIEF: Are you making fun of me? I don't know nothing about credentials or fucking official status. The only thing I do, is take orders. When we meet the General you can show him anything you want; but I'm going to tell you that the General knows what he's doing.

H: Okay, I showed you my credentials. May I see yours, please?

(The Chief takes him by the face and says with a menacing sweetness.)

CHIEF: Whaddayou gain by provoking me . . . being smacked around . . . or better yet, what if I leave my subordinate here with your horny wife? *(He notices the sub is missing.)* . . . Now where did that asshole go?

(In the bathroom we hear the woman screaming. H runs to the door, followed by the Chief. They enter. The shouts and violence increase. The Chief appears carrying the woman and throws her on the bed.)

WIFE: Savages! Beasts! Animals!

(The violence continues in the bathroom. The sub appears, his face bleeding. He is dragging H. He hits him. The Chief intercedes.)

CHIEF: Will ya stop already!

SUBORDINATE: He kicked me in the face! . . . in my face. Chief.

CHIEF: It's your fault. You were fucking with his wife.

SUBORDINATE: She pushed me.

H: All this will be brought to light! Bullies! Over a hundred people work with me. I have contacts at the highest levels. Even though you kidnap me. Everything will be known tomorrow. The minute I don't arrive at my office, the phone calls will begin. In just a few hours this house will fill with reporters, officials and intellectuals demanding an immediate investigation. You'll see, you slime, they'll even sic the army on you!

(The Chief kneels and takes him by the neck.)

CHIEF: It's best you shut up, sweetheart. You're not improving your situation the least bit. So you think a lot of people are going to look for you? Why would they look for you — they'll all know exactly where you are. We'll leave your old lady so she can tell the reporters and the hundred people from your office — although maybe your wife won't really want to tell them that you were thrown in jail, eh?

H: *(Afraid.)* In jail? They'll put me in jail for a crime I didn't commit?

CHIEF: No. We're going to put you in jail for one you did commit.

(He drags him to the window.) Look, look up there. As high as you can. That's where the order came from. So what do you think — are you guilty or not? And instead of standing there complaining, you should be grateful that they sent us, you imbecile, or you'd already be dead. Okay, now — you wanna see your arrest order?

(He takes out a wrinkled piece of paper. He signs it and puts it in H's pocket.)

CHIEF: There you have it for your records — what else do you want? You wanna talk on the phone . . . to the police?

(He brings the phone over to H and throws it at him.)

CHIEF: The station number is 53 . . . would you like me to dial it?

(He dials it. We hear a voice through the receiver.)

VOICE: Police station, may I help you?

CHIEF: Go ahead, I've got 'em on the line. Tell them your problems — while I go water the lilies.

(He goes to the bathroom. We hear the operator's voice insisting —)

VOICE: Hello . . . Hello . . .Police, can I help you? . . . this is the police station . . .

(The voice continues. H looks at the sub who is examining his bloody teeth in a mirror; at his wife who is watching him anxiously, and finally he hangs up the phone without saying anything.)

(His wife breaks down and sobs helplessly.)

(The lights dim.)

SCENE TWO: In the Holding Cells

A bunch of prostitutes, transvestites, drunks and criminals arrive, enlivening the gloominess of the police holding cells. Some are led into the jail proper; others — an actor with dyed hair and an umbrella, a gangbanger dressed like Rambo, a sleazy nightclub singer and a group of farmers — remain at the front desk to plead their cases.

CO-OP FARMER: No sir. You've got it wrong. We're agronomists not agressors. Farmers, sir . . .

ACTOR: This is a fluke, a scandal. I am an actor, a famous actor, German Robles. You must know who I am. My name's on all the billboards, the magazines. How is it possible that the simple fact of carrying an umbrella has made these four uniformed gorillas practically beat me to a pulp? . . .

GANGBANGER: Because, right, I was fed up with that bitch, always at me with "Ay son, you're not dressed warm enough," "Ay son, don't play your music so loud" . . . and yesterday, when I was leaving she comes out with I can't use the fucking TV. That pissed me off — so I went to the hardware store . . .

ACTOR: But I'd only walked two blocks from the theater and was about to have supper at the Konditori, taking advantage of a break in the play, when I feel them grab me by the neck, shouting, "Let's pull in this faggot with the umbrella too . . ."

NIGHTCLUB PERFORMER: Ah, no, whore, no. I'm a nightclub performer. That's my profession. Here, look at my card from the actor's guild, my health insurance card, payment receipts from police headquarters so I can turn . . . I mean so that I can work . . .

CO-OP FARMER: Because we work hard in the fields and we never had a problem with the law. Here — the only thing we were doing was selling our peanuts in the mall . . .

NIGHTCLUB PERFORMER: It was so near the nightclub that I didn't think there was anything wrong. A client complained of not feeling well so I helped him out and accompanied him to his car . . . .

GANGBANGER: And that was where I hid the machete. Later at night, I climbed a tree near her bedroom window, with the machete in my mouth and jumped to the balcony. I stayed there hours waiting for that hag to fall asleep . . .

NIGHTCLUB PERFORMER: Yeah, but instead of lying down to rest for a minute like the bastard told me, seeing that I was defenseless and alone, he dragged me inside the car and there I was a victim of this pervert when the officers jumped us . . .

CO-OP FARMER: And then they began to toss all our peanuts in the trunk — imagine that! Well, I couldn't stand it and I pitched a stone at one of their backs!

ACTOR: Guildenstein — Hamlet's friend, that's the character I portray in the play, since he's a Dane, I had to color my hair blond like the Danes. And since they're not dark-skinned like I am, but very white, I also had to put on make-up . . . .

(H enters escorted by the police agents. They sit him on a bench next to a little old lady. From there he listens to the following dialogues which are spoken in unison:)

CO-OP FARMER: But we're not agressors, we're agronomists! How many times do we have to say it! Farmers, agronomists, not agressors! Farmers . . . etc.

ACTOR: It's just that you don't know anything about theater or you'd understand my situation. Tomorrow we have an opening. A premiere. This you can understand, no? A Premiere. Even the secretary of education is invited. You can't lock me up for the whole weekend!

NIGHTCLUB PERFORMER: Have a heart, I have two daughters — one's a newborn. If you lock me up, who will feed them? Besides what crime have I committed? I'm an actress . . . I've always voted for whoever my congressman told me . . .

GANGBANGER: Then I gave it to her — again and again — like this! Wham, wham — just like in the Rambo pictures — wham! Wham! The old lady tried to get up, but I jumped from the night stand to the bed and then I lifted her by the hair — wham! Wham! Until she didn't move. Wham Wham!

(They freeze. Various police officers enter and take them away. On the bench next to him a grimy little old lady is knitting a ski cap. She is enjoying this.)

LITTLE OLD LADY: Those boys, those boys, always the same complaints, the same uproar — and, I ask you, why? It never works.

(H looks at her puzzled, her presence doesn't seem to fit. The old lady continues her comments.)

LITTLE OLD LADY: Although, of course, no one likes to be dragged in here. *(To H.)* Don't you agree?

H: Eh? Oh! Yes.

LITTLE OLD LADY: *(Knitting.)* It's all so ugly. But, with time, they get used to it.

H: Do you come here often?

LITTLE OLD LADY: Oh yes, every day . . . ever since . . . well quite a long time now. My two sons were in here. I used to come early to bring them things to eat and to be near them. Now I come, I don't know why . . . habit perhaps . . . my two sons died.

(Tears have filled her eyes and H loans her a handkerchief. The lady wipes her eyes and her nose.)

LITTLE OLD LADY: The guards already know me. They let me be. Actually I have no-where else to go. I don't like the room where I live, it's cold and doesn't have much light. Here it's warm and there's people. Time doesn't pass so slowly.

H: You said your two sons died?

LITTLE OLD LADY: Yes. They killed my oldest when he was trying to escape. It was a very famous case. His photo was in all the papers. My other son, they drowned in a toilet.

H: A toilet?

LITTLE OLD LADY: Yes. He couldn't stand the torture.

H: *(Uneasy.)* Torture?

LITTLE OLD LADY: You know — what they do to people who won't confess. It's very ugly. You should have seen my son when they gave him back to me — Oh! How they left his testicles. They looked like shriveled prunes, hanging by a black thread of skin, no wider than a shoelace, and his anus — I can't even imagine what they found to do back there.

H: *(In horror.)* All this for not confessing?

LITTLE OLD LADY: My youngest son wasn't a criminal, he was a mechanic, so when they accused him of being an accessory to a robbery, he rebelled and wouldn't confess a thing. That got them so furious with him . . . if he'd only done what his brother did, who confessed after the first few blows, they wouldn't have wounded him so . . .

H: But this is illegal! . . . torture . . . and You? . . . Didn't you file a lawsuit?

LITTLE OLD LADY: That doesn't do any good. Just imagine — according to the doctors he died from peritonitis, when the truth is that with all the compressed air forced in his rectum, they exploded everything inside him . . . *(A guard passes and smiles.)*

GUARD: How are you doin' old lady? Here so early?

LITTLE OLD LADY: You betcha, Mr. Guard.

(The old lady dries her tears, feels better and shows the guard the ski cap she's making.)

LITTLE OLD LADY: I'm working as fast as I can so I can have your ski cap ready before Christmas.

GUARD: What a great lady. You spoil us, really . . . *(He exits.)*

LITTLE OLD LADY: That's the head guard. Very energetic, very tough.

H: But how can you greet, how can you even tolerate these men after what they did to your sons?

LITTLE OLD LADY: They're good people. They were only doing their duty.

H: They murdered them. You yourself just told me, and in a vicious way . . . that's doing their duty?!

LITTLE OLD LADY: It's just their way of doing things. Not always the way one would want, but after all, they are the law.

H: No — they're not the law. They represent the law — but when they torture and murder, when they violate the most elemental human rights, we as citizens, have the right and the obligation to denounce them!

(The old lady looks at him, worried.)

LITTLE OLD LADY: Tell me son — what are you doing here?

H: I . . . I've also been arrested.

LITTLE OLD LADY: Jesus Christ! And that's what you're going to say when they interrogate you?

H: They haven't even let me contact my lawyer. Until I do, I won't say one word.

LITTLE OLD LADY: *(Heavy with meaning.)* You better talk to them, son. What are you accused of?

H: That's the thing. I don't know. But I'm innocent!

LITTLE OLD LADY: *(Alarmed.)* No. No. Don't say that to them! Better — declare yourself guilty right from the start!

H: Guilty of what?

LITTLE OLD LADY: Of whatever. They'll make you admit to everything anyway. No one can stand the torture. Even my youngest understood that — but too late — and he was a mechanic, really built, you're very delicate. I don't think you're going to tolerate very much!

(Terrified, H stands up and begins to speak, almost to himself.)

H: No. I won't let them torture me. I can't stand physical pain. I'm not made for it . . . I'll confess, yes I'll confess whatever they want. Anything before they hurt me!

LITTLE OLD LADY: That's very good.

H: Sooner or later the truth will come to light!

(At the back the lead guard appears. He shouts.)

GUARD: Hey you in the striped suit, to the bars!

LITTLE OLD LADY: There you go. They're talking to you. Don't dawdle.

H: It was a blessing meeting you. I wouldn't have known what to do otherwise.

LITTLE OLD LADY: You were very confused. You'll see — they're not so bad if you give a little. Let me bless you.

(He kneels and the old lady blesses him. H kisses her hand and leaves. The guard comes up to the old lady.)

GUARD: So how did it go Grandma?

LITTLE OLD LADY: *(Winking at him.)* He'll confess anything you want.

GUARD: You are a clever cunt, old lady. By the way — they're giving out paychecks now.

(The old lady is happy. She takes the guard's arm and they exit the scene laughing and joking.)

(Blackout.)

SCENE THREE: The Torturer

In the dark we hear cries and screams.

H: Ayyyy! . . . Ayyyyy! . . . please God — no more . . . ayyyy!
   (Half nude, with his back to us, H is hanging by his hands. His body shows evidence of the torture he's sustained. A little man, armed with a battery and car cable, connects them to different parts of H's body. H squirms like a worm. While the little man is checking the power on his apparatus, H complains.)
H: Why are you hurting me? . . . I already signed the confession. I even signed the blank forms . . . Plus I'll confess anything else you ask me to.
TORTURER: You're the fifth guy this week to babble everything before we even touch him. This is bad for our department. They're going to think we're not necessary and with all the budget cuts . . . they'll tell us to go to the devil. So take it you bastard, at least I'm treating you with great consideration!
   (He takes a bottle of mineral water and pours it up his nose.)
H: Ayyyy! . . . .Ayyyyy!
   (We still hear H's moans in the dark.)
   (Blackout.)

SCENE FOUR: The Professor

Two guards drag H down a corridor. He looks beaten and pitiful. They reach the cell and shove him in and exit. H feels along the floor until he comes to a moldy, lumpy cot that smells like stale sweat. He gets up on it and lies down sobbing for a time. Soon the repeated sound of a squeaking noise above his head makes him alert. He gets up and sees an unusually tall man with white hair calculating the physical properties of the cell and writing down mathematical formulas on the wall with chalk. The man comments worriedly.

PROFESSOR: A seven point five earthquake and we'll be fucked.
   (He sits. He takes out a bottle of soda, shakes it, taps the cap a couple of times, one twist, and the bottle opens easily. H observes this with admiration.)
PROFESSOR: Fucking buildings — The Department of Agriculture must have designed it! *(He offers H some soda, but H declines.)* And its reinforced with iron, probably too much and in all the wrong places. For less money they could have used tridiloza, and built a more functional and secure prison

. . . as if they give a fuck. I bet though, that that's just what they want — another earthquake so that all this shit falls on our heads and then they can blame mother nature for the disappearance of all the political prisoners!

H: *(Interested.)* Political prisoners?

PROFESSOR: Yes.

H: You mean . . . everyone here's a political prisoner?

PROFESSOR: At least those in this section, yes . . . you didn't know that? *(H shakes his head. A pause.)* What did you think you were?

H: I dunno. They haven't told me yet.

(The Professor cleans his glasses and looks at him more intently.)

PROFESSOR: You haven't been told what crime you committed?

H: *(Quickly.)* I haven't committed any crime — least of all political! I mean . . . I haven't participated in any anti-governmental activities, or gone against any of my Party's decisions in any way. I'm what you could call a Convinced Institutionalist.

PROFESSOR: *(Laughs.)* Yeah, you're a subversive. And now I know who you are. *(The Professor digs in his clothes and pulls out a wrinkled newspaper. He checks to make sure the guards aren't around and begins to read it.)*

PROFESSOR: "The moralization campaign continues. A high official, arrested yesterday, it seems, for the crime of embezzlement."

H: *(Livid.)* That refers to me?

(H almost tears it out of the Professor's hand. The lines of his face harden as he reads it.)

H: This can't be. This is monstrous . . . lies. I have to speak with my lawyer! *(He throws himself against the bars.)* Guards! Get me out of here! You can't hold me incommunicado while they're out there covering my name with infamous lies! I demand a lawyer! . . . guards! . . . guards!

PROFESSOR: Calm down. You won't fix anything that way. They'll just fuck you up all over again.

H: This isn't just! This isn't fair! . . . How could they do this to me? They're destroying my life!

PROFESSOR: There, there it's not all that bad.

(H comes apart on the cot. The Professor tries to calm him.)

PROFESSOR: Really, why torture yourself this way. After all, this government will go to hell soon.

H: Ten years of total loyalty to the Party.

PROFESSOR: Its lack of ability to govern the country and its level of corruption are already intolerable everyone agrees.

H: Ten years holding true to the idea of service.

PROFESSOR: The violence in the universities is only a reflection of the general unrest in the country, of the crisis in the countryside, the disapproval in the factories.

(The Professor's words are illustrated by film or slides from the events of 1968. When the exhibit has ended, the two men are in the dining room getting their food. The Professor continues his indoctrination.)

PROFESSOR: They've only been able to keep themselves in power by taking out so many loans, but now they can't even pay the interest on their external debt; and moreover, the World Bank knows that a people's government isn't going to pay them this money — which the people never asked for and which can't be found anywhere in the country anyway. So, they won't be able to get more loans. On the other hand, our historic political processes, which are inexorable . . .

(Film or slides of the Mexican Revolution. At the end of these the men are doing exercises in the patio.)

PROFESSOR: The conditions are given. The only thing missing is the detonator and we have it — a political party — that really represents the workers!

H: A political party? . . . Here?

PROFESSOR: Why right here we have experience from the peasants' struggle; the workers' unions, our university students. We haven't just sat here with our arms crossed while conflicts are boiling over on the outside.

(They've arrived at the cell. The Professor discretely confides in him.)

PROFESSOR: That's why they have us locked up, because they're afraid of us, because they know that as soon as we're out of here, their days are numbered.

(We begin to hear a lot of noise in the patio.)

PROFESSOR: *(Frightened.)* Oh shit. They've let them loose again!

H: Who?

PROFESSOR: The regular prisoners. Hide anything you have of value. Hide yourself!

H: *(Alarmed.)* But . . . why?

PROFESSOR: Don't ask. Hide wherever you can!

(They have no time. A mass of subhumans that seem to have escaped from a painting by Bosch violently appears and in the least time imaginable beats H and the Professor, takes away all their clothes and belongings, and also rapes H. He remains hysterical, shouting through the thick bars.)

(Black Out.)

Scene Five: At the Airport

H's wife and son are being sent off. The wife cries in her mother's arms. The son plays on the ground with a little car. The father comes and pulls his daughter aside.

PAPA: So how is your family situation? Did your husband finally agree to the divorce?

WIFE: Rafa . . . my lawyer . . . did a splendid job.

PAPA: And even though there's only speculation about what crime your "ex" has actually committed, I must warn you that in cases of embezzlement, the law is obliged to confiscate everything he's acquired and sometimes that means they move against his personal belongings as well.

WIFE: I already sold the house and all the furniture. I also cleaned out our bank accounts. At first I was reluctant to take all the money, but Rafa . . . my lawyer, says we don't have the right to gamble with our son's future.

PAPA: And he's right.

WIFE: He thinks that if my ex is innocent, they'll reinstate him in the government, and if not, well, whatever he took with him should be enough for him to live on.

PAPA: And you? What do you think? Is he guilty?

W: I don't want to think about it. I've suffered a lot. People tell so many versions of what happened — everything from his being a populist to hooking up with a stripper who was exploiting him.

PAPA: What a jerk!

WIFE: *(She can't help but laugh.)* Ay, Papa, that last one. I don't believe. Poor thing. I wonder what he's doing now . . .
(The lights fade on this area of the stage.)

Scene Six: Visiting Day at the Prison

Crowded around the bars, the prisoners are showered with food, gifts and affection by their families.

H remains alone and isolated in his cell, without visitors or love. After saying good-bye to his wife, the Professor goes to H and puts his arm around his shoulders trying to console him. He invites H to share a little of his recently acquired cake.

The lights fade in this area.

Scene Seven

The lights come up at the airport.

WIFE: Well, in spite of all the pain he's caused us, I don't wish him ill. I hope he gets out of there soon.

PAPA: *(Alarmed.)* Of course if he gets out, you two aren't going to . . .

WIFE: After all I've suffered . . . no Papa . . . *(She cries.)* . . . That's why I'm leaving — to see if I can put my life back together.

PAPA: And if it's not too indiscrete to ask, why Spain?

WIFE: For my son . . . he loves flamenco music!

VOICEOVER: Passengers for flight 304, with destination to Korea, Guayaquil and Barcelona — please go to gate 37.

(This is repeated in Korean, Spanish, Catalan and Equadorian.)
(The wife turns to wave to her family while the lights fade . . .)
(Black Out.)

Scene Eight: The Lawyer

H is sleeping in his cell. He's begun to look dirty and neglected. A discrete "Ahem" interrupts his insipid dream. He turns and sees a short, plump, sweaty man, moving nervously in front of him. When their eyes meet, the lawyer smiles showing a couple of empty spaces among his teeth. He's wearing a checkered jacket and a T-shirt that says "I love Vail" and wide pants tucked into colored tennis shoes.

H: Who are you?

LAWYER: Your lawyer, sir.

H: *(Apathetic.)* Another one?

LAWYER: Mr. Alardea gave up your case, sir.

H: Him too? That little devil didn't even tell me. That makes three.

LAWYER: I volunteered.

H: *(Without looking at him.)* Do you know why they all quit?

LAWYER: I believe it was a question of location.

H: Location?

LAWYER: They were all from the suburbs.

H: Yeah?

LAWYER: A question of prestige, sir. Yours is a lost case. They weren't going to risk their reputations.

H: How can they know my case is lost when they can't even find out what I'm accused of?!

LAWYER: In the media — it's not a question of what you're accused of, but who is doing the accusing!

H: So you mean, in my case, the "who" who has accused me, leaves me with no possible defense?

LAWYER: Well with the lawyers from the suburbs . . . yes . . . *(Rapidly.)* But I'm from the inner city.

H: So you'll take this lost case?

LAWYER: It's a financial question, sir. My situation is really shitty. I owe three months rent, and my wife has a newborn.

H: What? The milkman doesn't help you with the rent?

LAWYER: I don't understand.

H: I'm sorry. I don't know what made me say that . . . It's a reflex answer. I guess . . . maybe I'm so weak I've become delirious. I don't know, but I insist you forgive me. It was a terrible joke!

LAWYER: Oh. Oh! *(He laughs heartily.)*

H: Please don't feel obligated to laugh. The joke was stupid and out of line. What may interest you, however, is to analyze how, despite all these days of suffering, I've even felt the impulse to tell a joke. Before, yes, I used to joke a lot. My employees enjoyed my humor, they always made me stand up so I'd tell a few. They said I had very good timing . . . but now . . . your presence here . . . forgive me.

LAWYER: It was an excellent joke and very timely, sir.

H: Depends on your humor. So! What are we doing here?

LAWYER: I'm going to take your case.

H: Because you're starving?

LAWYER: Among other things.

H: At least you're honest. But there's something that doesn't jell; you said my case is lost.

LAWYER: And so it is.

H: Then I don't need a lawyer.

LAWYER: Well, I believe there's a chance. It's a question of focus. I'm not going to prove your innocence — that would be awkward, useless and expensive.

H: So?

LAWYER: Taking advantage that the possibility of embezzlement has only been suggested, my efforts will be directed towards minimizing your crime.

H: *(Ironic.)* I see, you'll show me to be a criminal on a small scale or should we say a petty criminal?

LAWYER: Sir, listen to me. You're not innocent. You can't be. That's clear, but we could look to have you pardoned, or at least that you receive the most benevolent sentence possible.

(H is beginning to be interested in this little man who's sweating as if he were in a sauna.)

H: That makes sense.

LAWYER: Our first step will be to get you out of here on bond, so that we can make an appeal to your friends.

H: Which friends? Everyone I contacted refused to answer my calls.

LAWYER: You're right. Perhaps this isn't the best forum to test your friendships.

H: Well, we could try it.

(The crucial moment has arrived. The lawyer wipes the sweat from his brow with his sleeve, takes a breath and plunges in.)

LAWYER: What I am going to require, and this is only an advance, and not only to post bond but also so that your servant along with his family can have a hot meal tonight . . .

H: I'll make out a check.

(The lawyer smiles happily.)

(Black Out.)

SCENE NINE: The Escape

Early morning in the north wing of the prison. A shadow crosses the corridors and stops in front of a cell. It is the Professor. He makes a sharp sound with his lips. H hears the signal and wakes up. He comes to the bars.

H: What's happening?

PROFESSOR: Pack your things. We're getting out of here in one hour.

H: In . . . in an hour? . . . where are you going?

PROFESSOR: To the hills, right now. Everything's ready. Fourteen of us are going, fifteen with you.

(This is an option H hasn't considered. He's full of doubts.)

H: But, just like that? I don't know. I have to think it over.

PROFESSOR: So think about it. You have forty-five seconds!

H: How are you going to do it?

PROFESSOR: In the laundry truck. We bought two guards. They're taking care of everything.

H: Well . . . what's happening is that I've already . . . I'm about to get out. I spoke with my lawyer just yesterday. He says they'll let me out on bail. Once I'm out I can clear everything up.

PROFESSOR: *(Impatient.)* They're not going to give you bail and you're not going to be able to clear things up. Are you blind? Look, for some reason that you don't even know about, you've become an enemy of the system. That's why they have you here and they're hoping to keep you here until you rot!

H: It's that if I get out by legal means, I'll be able to lead a normal life and rescue my name and honor.

PROFESSOR: A normal life? In this rotten society? Please! With us, you'll have the chance to change all this shit, at least to attempt it!

H: *(Suddenly intense.)* To change it into what? Don't you understand. I've dedicated my whole life, all my talents to my party. I wouldn't know what to do with you guys. I wouldn't be of any use to you!

PROFESSOR: Your political experience could be of great use to us!

H: In all this time we've lived together, I've come to understand your ideas and to value them, and I have great respect for you, but the truth is, with you guys I'd be like an old nun who you're trying to convince that God doesn't exist.

PROFESSOR: God doesn't exist! And your party has liquidated you! Be reborn with us!

H: I'm with you but from the only trenches I know.

PROFESSOR: That isn't a trench. It's a swamp. A sewer!

H: Sometimes conditions change. My whole attitude will be different if I'm given another chance. This time in jail . . . having gotten to know you . . . I'll try to change things.

(There's a long pause. The Professor looks at his watch.)

PROFESSOR: All right. It's your decision.

H: I'll be waiting to hear about you guys and everything you accomplish.

PROFESSOR: Sure, if they don't fuck you before.

H: Let's hope not.

PROFESSOR: *(Smiles.)* Dream on — partner.

H: Give 'em hell, Maestro.

(They embrace through the bars. The light dims.)

Scene Ten: A Letter From His Mother

My dear son: How good it was to get your letter after so long and how terrible to learn that you've been in the North Prison. What a horrible experience, even though you're only there because of a misunderstanding. Hopefully you haven't gotten sick to your stomach. You're so delicate, and try not to go around barefoot. They say that jails are very cold. You don't know how badly I'd like to help you the way I used to when you were little, do you remember? But now that I'm old and sick and so far away, there's little I can do.

About the money you asked me for, son, I don't know how to tell you this, but everything is so expensive. I had to spend all the money you left me. The truth is, I wasn't sure if I was supposed to keep it for you or if you gave it to me in order to help your ancient mother. I have very little left. It's that your father's pension doesn't reach very far these days. However, if you need the money so desperately, you can have the house. You can sell it. I'm going to die soon anyway. In the meantime, you can put me in an old folks home — because there's no sacrifice that a mother wouldn't make for her son.

What I don't understand is about your lawyer; You contract him to defend you and now he's suing you too? Why did you give him a check without funds? You know how litigious those lawyers are.

Also, your divorce surprised me. I feel so badly for your son and you. But then you know what I always thought of your wife — she was a shallow bitch who married you for your money. I told you that many times! And I can't forget that it was because of her that you grew so distant from me after I forbid you to put her name on anything you had of value. I hope you'll pay attention to me now, and with such a hard lesson that life has given you, you'll realize that your mother always told you to do what was good for you.

(Her voice fades out. Lights up on the prison. H is reading his mother's letter in his cell when two guards enter and without saying a word they tie his hands and feet.)

H: And now, what have I done? *(The guards begin to strip him. H is terrified.)* No, please God . . . not again! No! . . .
(They struggle with him and he resists but the guards succeed in stripping off his clothes. Then they dress him in clean pants and a white t-shirt. H calms down. The men put a tennis racquet in his hand and take him away.)
(Blackout.)

SCENE ELEVEN: On the Tennis Court

An excellent clay tennis court where H and Big Shot play a hard fought set of tennis.

> *Big Shot is a distinguished-looking man who the guards, now dressed in loud Hawaiian shirts and shorts, applaud enthusiastically each time his ball goes over the net. At last, a strong passing shot ends the set and the guards receive both players with towels. As they wipe their faces, Big Shot says:*

BIG SHOT: You play very well. I had to use all my strength and technique.

H: Your forehand is amazing. I couldn't get a handle on it.

> *(They go to a table set especially for them and sit down. The guards serve them with great solicitude.)*

BIG SHOT: Would you like a drink?

H: A beer, thanks.

BIG SHOT: Get me a whiskey with mineral water.

> *(Big Shot takes out a cigar, which the guard lights for him. The other hurries to serve the drinks.)*

BIG SHOT: It's been enjoyable playing with you. My instructor got sick. I didn't want to stop practicing. You'll forgive me if I sent for you?

H: I'm very grateful. I've really enjoyed this game. It's been so long since I enjoyed anything. I'll sleep well tonight.

> *(Drinks and hor d'oeuvres are served. The guards stand at a prudent distance. They stand in attendance without hearing the conversation. Once in a while, they approach to serve something, change the ashtrays, etc.)*

BIG SHOT: How're things going?

H: Bad. There's complications.

BIG SHOT: But you're all right? Comfortable?

H: No. It's like an interminable nightmare.

BIG SHOT: I shouldn't have let them take you to the section for political prisoners. They're treated the worst.

H: How could you have stopped it?

BIG SHOT: By paying. Here everything is possible, if you pay.

> *(H watches the guards and they smile at him obsequiously.)*

H: Yes, I suppose you're right.

BIG SHOT: Things could still be arranged.

H: *(Ashamed.)* Unfortunately, I'm short of funds right now.

BIG SHOT: No? That is serious.

H: If I could get out of here. I could prove my innocence.

BIG SHOT: Innocence?

H: Of course. I never took the money that was entrusted to me, nor did I use any for my personal benefit.

BIG SHOT: Poorly done. That's why things have gone so badly for you.

H: I don't understand.

BIG SHOT: *(Smiles.)* My friend, you were an executive. At that level you should have understood that the system doesn't judge whether someone is honest or dishonest because of the simple act of taking out his own reward from the budget funds that are submitted for his approval. You see it's a matter of "the end justifying the means" and when it's toward our Party's end, every mechanism used to fortify it is justifiable.

H: Embezzling strengthens the Party?

BIG SHOT: It's always better when the party ranks are filled with individuals who enjoy a healthy financial level which gives them solvency and respectability. That makes them powerful, influential, convincing and effective. That's why they're given public office with all its possibilities at their disposal, so that they make full use of them, with circumspection, and yes, of course a certain cleverness that doesn't let it get out to the masses and then cause them to get unduly excited. *(Paternal.)* But no, my friend, I assure you that fraud has nothing to do with your arrest.

H: But then . . . the law of responsibility for public employees? What about all the arrests we've made for supposed frauds?

BIG SHOT: A little legal window-dressing used at our discretion because of the resonance it has for the public — its public opinion value. But if you really analyze it, an unblemished use of state functions or executive power would block the adequate flow of funds that the Party dynamic requires; its election campaigns; the constant propaganda, the immense cost of maintaining its bureaucratic paraphernalia, whose official budget, any one can see, is insufficient.

H: Then . . . then . . . what crime did I commit?

BIG SHOT: That's the first thing we should investigate!

H: But how? Where? I'm well acquainted with the internal legislation of the Party, its principles, and I can assure you that I never deviated from them. Never!

(Big Shot looks at him with sympathy.)

BIG SHOT: How long were you Director of The Film Institute?

H: Why?

BIG SHOT: Truthfully, it seems naive of you to think decisions by the State would be based on legal statutes, when there's a whole body of unwritten law, as ample and accessible as you please, which authorizes all the possibilities that power may provide.

(H has remained astonished. Big Shot continues.)

BIG SHOT: My friend, don't you understand that if a superior merely changes his mind he can change how policies are carried out, even a change in moral tone is enough to alter circumstances without prior notice. One can find oneself outside the magic circle, or even outside the social order, as happened with me, by a mere whim or flick of a pen.

H: But what you're describing can't be . . . it would be monstrous . . . individual integrity depends on unwritten laws?

BIG SHOT: The integrity of the whole country is subjected to these unwritten laws.

(Big Shot lifts his empty glass. A guard refills it for him.)

BIG SHOT: You tell me — where's the Party statute that authorizes the president to determine his successor? What article of the Constitution allows the president to decide one morning, in the privacy of his bedroom, that the State will expropriate all the banks in the country? From there on down, the unwritten law opens like a Pandora's Box, corrupting at all levels and in every public act. Each new president will dictate his own six-year legislation, and as barbarous as it sounds, the official just below him will obey blindly and irrationally, but with great political acumen. Do you understand me?

H: Yes. I believe I do.

BIG SHOT: Accept the idea that this is the way things are, and how they'll always be and search out the point where your work ethic broke with the system. That's the only way you'll find out where you went wrong. Plus you'll have a chance to realign yourself with the powers that be and be vindicated!

H: I thought that if I succeeded in getting out, I'd look for the Señora who was my boss.

BIG SHOT: That would be a terrible blunder. She probably wouldn't agree to see you. Even worse, she'd keep you hanging and you'd lose precious time. But even if she did receive you, what would you say to her? How would you argue in your defense without knowing what the charge against you was?

H: She could tell me what it was.

BIG SHOT: Never! My friend — your arrest could have been the result of a personal whim, or it could be the result of some complicated political maneuver that the Señora would never discuss with you. No. First, find out!

Get all the information that you can and figure out your line of defense, if there is one. Then, yes, when the time is right, when it's prudent, lay out all your cards on the table. *(He looks at H.)* But hey — why so discouraged?

H: *(Beaten.)* It's that I don't even know where to begin.

BIG SHOT: *(Discretely.)* There's someone here who can help you. He's not a party member, but he has great influence inside prison and also within the country's judicial system.

H: Why is he here?

BIG SHOT: Because he's a patriot. He nationalized the drug industry and attacked the CIA. They obliged our authorities to lock him up. However, he still has great power. It's not the type of friendship that gives social prestige, but it can be very convenient — especially in cases like your own. If you'd like, I can try to get you in to see him. Maybe he can help you.

H: Well, yes. That would interest me. How can I reach him?

BIG SHOT: Leave that to me.

(He snaps his fingers at the guards.)

BIG SHOT: Accompany him.

(H starts to go, but something's turning over in his mind and he stops. He turns to Big Shot and asks him confidentially . . .)

H: If this is too personal, you don't have to answer, but how much do you pay for all this?

(Big Shot whispers something in his ear.)

H: A month?

BIG SHOT: A day.

(H exits talking to himself. Big Shot comments to himself . . .)

BIG SHOT: Yep. I'm a big shot . . .

(Finishes his whiskey and goes to take a nap.)

(Blackout.)

SCENE TWELVE

A cell decorated with an oriental motif. The Capo sits nestled into pillows underneath a canopy of striped canvas and hung with Persian rugs. He is a small, mannered man, with a high voice, who is inhaling smoke from some sort of peace pipe with various attachments. He is wearing a silk robe and is paying close attention to the bobbing breasts and hips of a semi-nude exotic dancer who is wearing a costume that seems to have been taken out of a Hawaiian luau. She does a Persian dance to a sinuous rhythm.

Two armed guards enter, escorting H. One of them indicates where he should sit, the other offers him a mouthpiece from the pipe. H smokes. He is surprised by the taste of the smoke. He asks the guard what it is. The guard whispers something in his ear, after which H discretely puts the pipe aside.

After a crescendo that the exotic dancer attacks with great enthusiasm, the number ends. The sweaty dancer stands in front of the boss waiting for applause that doesn't come. The girl lifts her gaze and her fear increases, seeing that the little man is sitting there with no expression. All of a sudden as if he were waking up, he smiles and orders.)

CAPO: She'll be in the movie.
(The girl is overcome with joy and almost loses her balance, tripping over H who doesn't know how to react. After a moment trying to dodge breasts, legs and buttocks, H decides to withdraw.)

H: With your permission . . . good night.
(On hearing his voice, the Capo turns and stares at H as if he had just invented him. He smiles. He moves the exotic dancer to one side.)

CAPO: Put her in my bed!
(The guards take the dancer away, the Capo nods at H and indicates that H should sit next to him.)

H: If you'll let me explain.

CAPO: It's not necessary, I know all about it. Including, I already know who can give you the information you're looking for.

H: Who?

CAPO: *(Smiles.)* I also arranged for your bail.
(H's face lights up at the prospect of his freedom.)

CAPO: You'll get out on Tuesday afternoon. Now, when you go back to your cell, you'll find a little package under your pillow. It's the clothes you should put on to contact our agent and some instructions. A code melody is mentioned there — it goes like this:
(He whistles "For He's a Jolly Good Fellow.")

CAPO: Now you.

H: I got it.
(He whistles it to the Capo's satisfaction.)

CAPO: Enough. Good. There's not much time so I recommend that you act with precision.

H: I'll remember that, sir. I'll take that into account.

CAPO: You're in a big mess, but I'll get you out of it. You'll see.

H: Some day I'll pay you back for everything you've done for me.

CAPO: Yes, my men will tell you how.

(H remains thoughtful, trying to understand the meaning of this last phrase. The Capo smiles at him enigmatically. Finally H exits. A man wrapped in a black raincoat follows him.)

(Blackout.)

END OF ACT ONE

ACT TWO
SCENE ONE: On the City Streets

Some part of Mexico City. Cars piled up on the street and the curbs. Dried bird droppings on trees, lights and cables. Angry people trying to cross the street while a concert of horns, curses and commercial announcements invades a sky black with smog and fumes from Texcocan shit.

We hear the sound of a motorcycle, someone braking rapidly. A Traffic Cop walks up to a car, taking off his gloves.

TRAFFIC COP: You went through a stop sign, sir.

DRIVER: A stop sign? Where?

TRAFFIC COP: Don't play dumb. I've been following you since the viaduct.

DRIVER: I see, you've got the wrong car. I didn't come that way.

TRAFFIC COP: *(Without seeming to hear him.)* Your speed got my attention. You almost wiped out an old lady.

DRIVER: Me?

(The policeman takes out his notebook and writes something down.)

TRAFFIC COP: Breathe out.

DRIVER: Why?

TRAFFIC COP: *(Writing.)* Alcohol on his breath.

DRIVER: You're kidding! I haven't drunk anything since I had two beers last night.

TRAFFIC COP: We'll clear this up at the station.

DRIVER: What! Why the hell are you taking me to the station?

TRAFFIC COP: *(Writing.)* Speeding, ignoring a stop sign and alcohol on his breath — that's it.

DRIVER: But you know that's not true!

TRAFFIC COP: Of course it's true. I say so.

(Smiles.)

It's your word against mine. Show me your license please.

(The driver gives it to him. He is nervous. He checks his watch.)

DRIVER: Jesus Christ! It's late! Look, officer. I have to be at the airport before one to deliver some documents. It's very important! I beg you, give me a fine and let me go!

TRAFFIC COP: *(Studying the license.)* This isn't you.

DRIVER: What do you mean, it's not me?

TRAFFIC COP: Doesn't look like you.

DRIVER: Is that my fault!

TRAFFIC COP: Let's see your insurance card.

DRIVER: *(Impatient.)* What for?

(Very calmly, the policeman gets out a thick booklet.)

TRAFFIC COP: You'll permit me to read you the traffic code.

DRIVER: It's okay. It's fine. Here's some more identification.

TRAFFIC COP: *(Reading.)* "The driver is required to present the required documentation."

(His voice fades as does the light in his area. At the end of the street, H appears, dressed in the orange uniform of the DDE (street cleaner). He carries a bin with brooms inside. A man in a hurry approaches him.)

MAN: Excuse me, what time is it?

(H looks at him, smiles and whistles the code melody. The man stares at him surprised and goes on his way. H comes across the policeman and the driver and goes towards them. Seeing him, they stop their argument. H whistles the melody again. The traffic agent is annoyed and motions for H to move along. H moves away. The men continue arguing.)

DRIVER: My library card too? What the hell for?

TRAFFIC COP: *(Writing.)* Resisting arrest.

DRIVER: *(Furious.)* I'm not resisting arrest! I only asked you "what the hell for?"!

TRAFFIC COP: *(Writing.)* And using foul language.

(The driver looks at his watch and gets out of the car.)

DRIVER: Officer, can't we make some other arrangement?

TRAFFIC COP: After you've gotten me all upset?

DRIVER: I didn't mean to. I was in a hurry. Now I'm not. Let's figure this out.

(The policeman's attitude changes. He becomes friendly.)

TRAFFIC COP: Buddy — it looks bad. I'm not sure you have enough.

DRIVER: How much?

TRAFFIC COP: And you know, we can't fix this today — so you might have to spend the weekend in jail.

DRIVER: *(Stronger.)* How much!

TRAFFIC COP: And jail could be really bad for you — what with all the degenerates and you with your soft white skin.

DRIVER: *(Tough.)* Let's get this over with. How much?

TRAFFIC COP: *(Smiles.)* Well, look, in spite of our troubles here, I like you . . . so let's leave it at two big ones.

DRIVER: Two hundred dollars?!

TRAFFIC COP: Don't argue with me or I'll change my mind.

(The driver goes to his car and takes out a beige jacket. He takes out two bills and hands it over to the officer.)

TRAFFIC COP: Hey thanks! If you like, I could escort you to the airport. I'll even use my siren so you can get there faster.

(The driver puts on his jacket and checks his watch.)

DRIVER: What for? My plane left.

TRAFFIC COP: Well have a good day.

(He goes towards his motorcycle. The driver's voice stops him.)

DRIVER: One minute officer.

(The agent returns as the driver puts on a military cap.)

DRIVER: Would you be so kind as to show me your credentials?

TRAFFIC COP: My what?

DRIVER: *(Tough.)* Your military identity card . . . soldier!

(Still smiling, nervous, the policeman is hoping this is a joke.)

TRAFFIC COP: Very funny. See ya.

(He's about to get on his motorcycle when the military officer's voice and the sound of a pistol hammer being drawn back stops him.)

DRIVER: I wouldn't advise you to go against the authority of the Mexican Army!

(The policeman is frightened when he sees the pistol aimed at him.)

TRAFFIC COP: Whoa! Don't point that thing at me! I'm only a traffic cop.

DRIVER: You are a soldier, with the rights and duties given to you by military authority, and I as a captain in the army demand that you show me proof of military service. So, for the last time, show me your military service card.

TRAFFIC COP: *(Stuttering.)* Well I . . . I don't have it.

DRIVER: Ah no? Let me remind you that it's every citizen's duty to carry with him proof of having served in the military . . . and you don't have it with you? Well, I guess you'll just have to come with me to army headquarters.

TRAFFIC COP: *(In a panic.)* But . . . I was only doing my duty!

DRIVER: I don't think so . . . *(Smiles.)* and it's your word against mine.

(The driver grabs him and pushes him into the car.)

DRIVER: Go ahead dipshit, get in. You'll see how we treat smartass slackers.

(The driver leaves with the policeman.)

(The lights dim.)

SCENE TWO: The Contact

The coming and going of people on the street lessens. Only H remains and an ice cream man with his cart and some ladies from the neighborhood on the corner. Not seeing any prospect for contact, H sits down beside his trash bin and brooms to wait. One of the neighborhood women comes toward him.

NEIGHBOR WOMAN: Are you comfortable? Is the sun bothering you?

H: Huh?

NEIGHBOR WOMAN: If you like I could bring you an umbrella and a beach chair . . . perhaps a little coconut oil?

H: *(Thinking she's crazy.)* Very kind of you.

NEIGHBOR WOMAN: How about a nice cold beer . . . I suppose this is what they're paying you for, to come here and take a vacation!

(H doesn't understand such an absurd conversation, but it crosses his mind that this could be his contact. He whistles the code-sign. She looks at him astonished. H repeats the tune and the lady loses it and attacks him with a basket.)

NEIGHBOR WOMAN: I'm talking to you. Don't be fresh!

(Understands his mistake and stops his concertizing.)

H: Please, forgive me.

NEIGHBOR WOMAN: It's because of lazy bums like you that our country's going to the dogs.

H: If you'd just let me explain . . . I didn't know what you were talking to me about!

NEIGHBOR WOMAN: Can't you see the fly-infested dungheap, in front of the school? A breeding ground for infection for our children, and you, laying about, I've been watching you for awhile . . . *(She looks inside the trash bin.)* . . . Just as I thought; you haven't picked up even one piece of paper. What a farce!

(At last H understands her complaint and smiles, trying to explain.)

H: Look, what's going on is . . . *(Thinks better of it.)* You are right! I'm going to clean this street right away, I was distracted for a minute, that's all.

(He begins to sweep. The lady, satisfied, goes back to her friend and the two exit. The ice cream man comes over with his cart.)

ICE CREAM MAN: Stupid fucking nosey hag. Don't pay any attention to her.

(H looks at the ice cream man who ,with his idiot grin, is sucking on a popsicle.)

H: She's right. This street is a filthy mess.

(H is afraid that while this repulsive guy is near him, his contact won't dare approach. Discretely, he sweeps and tries to distance himself. The ice cream man follows him.)

ICE CREAM MAN: Wouldn't you like a popsicle?

H: No thanks.

ICE CREAM MAN: They're really good.

H: Yeah. I can see that, but I really don't feel like one right now.

(He continues sweeping and the ice cream man keeps following him.)

ICE CREAM MAN: I'll give it to you for nothin'.

H: I said no!

ICE CREAM MAN: The kind I got'll charge your batteries but good.

(H takes notice. There's something in the voice of this subhuman that he's not getting. He feels tempted to face the guy, but he looks so repulsive that he can't bring himself to do it. He continues sweeping. The ice cream man goes back to his cart, whistling. H reacts. In the far reaches of this guy's whistling he perceives the code tune. He leaves his bin and goes over to the ice cream man.)

H: Give me a popsicle!

ICE CREAM MAN: Tamarind or red currant?

H: Whatever!

(The ice cream man gives it to him. The two men look at each other and whistle, laughing.)

H: I was put off by your disguise.

ICE CREAM MAN: My what?

H: I was looking for someone different.

ICE CREAM MAN: Different than what?

(H is disconcerted. He looks at the imbecilic face of the ice cream man and changes his approach.)

H: It's not important. What are your instructions?

ICE CREAM MAN: Well get with it so you can start humpin'.

H: You mean . . . working?

ICE CREAM MAN: Jesus — selling popsicles.

H: I don't understand.

ICE CREAM MAN: What don't you understand?

H: Nothing! There must be some misunderstanding. I didn't come here to hump and especially not to sell popsicles!

ICE CREAM MAN: Yeah, but these are special. They're loaded. Like the one you're working on.

(H takes the popsicle out of his mouth and looks at this ice cream delicacy.)

H: *(Nervous.)* Why? What's inside it?

ICE CREAM MAN: It depends. Has your mouth begun to tingle?

H: It feels like my tongue's swelling.

ICE CREAM MAN: Don't worry, real soon you'll start feeling very relaxed.

H: *(Scared.)* What did you give me? Poison? Drugs?

(The ice cream man nods smiling.)

H: Oh my God. I've been drugged. What's going to happen to me?

ICE CREAM MAN: Nothing, man I gave you one of our family promotions.

H: Look, I'm not used to drugs. It'll do me harm.

ICE CREAM MAN: Stop whining. It's a kid's high.

H: You mean, you give this to kids?

ICE CREAM MAN: We gotta widen our clientele. They're our best market. You got to think of mañana, no?

H: *(Green.)* I think I'm going to vomit.

(The ice cream man tries to help him. H pushes him away.)

H: Don't touch me you monster — I'm not one of yours!

(He vomits, gets a hold of himself and starts to move away.)

H: If you think that to save my skin . . . I'm not going to participate in this criminal traffic! You've made a mistake with me! You're very mistaken if you think . . .

(Stumbles. He falls to the ground and hits his head. He remains there panting, with a gone look on his face. The ice cream man looks at him in disgust.)

ICE CREAM MAN: What kind of fucking idiot did they send me?

H: *(From the ground.)* Get away! Get away you miserable wretch!

ICE CREAM MAN: Get it together, man, before you really piss me off and I fucking throttle you. Right like what's the deal? I mean I could give a fuck whether you want to peddle this shit or not, but somehow you got to the Capo and I got to make the best of it.

(He takes some popsicles out of his cart.)

ICE CREAM MAN: Here's your quota and careful — this is hard stuff and very costly, sweetheart. For macho guys, pure jet-set, the kind that goes to school in El Chuco and come back with a real heavy habit.

(In the distance a man in a black raincoat appears.)

ICE CREAM MAN: One of these bitches, the one you're delivering the popsicles to, is niece of the old bag that set you up, but lips sealed, eh? You'll be her candyman and you can get out of her whatever you like.

(He gives H a wrinkled piece of paper.)

ICE CREAM MAN: Your instructions. I'm going to give you the monthly quota, so like, eyes open, bro and don't try to put one over on me or you'll end up taking a dive in the sewage ditch.

(He takes his little cart and leaves. H manages to get up and lean against a wall and stays there, watching the parade of pink and green elephants wavering throughout the street.)

(Blackout.)

SCENE THREE: In Hell

In the basement of a big old house. A party full of hip young people dressed like American musicians — the Sioux-punk, the Cholos, a bunch of Kiss look-alikes, Alice Cooper doubles, heavy metal musicians and other famous singers and heavy rock groups. Their outfits are both expensive and aggressive.

The scene looks like a dance club on American TV. No tables or chairs, only pillows scattered around a carpeted floor where young people are drinking, making out, or simply listening to the music and fooling around. Thick smoke with spots of colored light indirectly contributes to the hellish effect of this youth scene.

At the back is a more intimate and private space where people enter and exit, usually in couples. Most of the young people are about seventeen years old.

After a riff on drums and percussions, a small area lights up, suggestive of a huge television screen where we see three young girls singing.

TRIO: Forget your inhibitions, indulge your predilections.
Forget your inhibitions, indulge your predilections.
Forget your inhibitions, indulge your predilections.
Jazz yourself, smoke yourself, shoot a little smack
Then fuck whoever's near you down the throat or up their crack.
The world's going to end and we are never coming back.

Sooo —
Forget your inhibitions, indulge your predilections.
etc.

Flee your schools, leave your job, set yourself on fire
It's just blackness that awaits us so let's start by getting higher
Cause if we're gonna die, why wait til we retire?
Forget your inhibitions . . . etc.

Watch your folks, check your back, take a look around

Cuz what's coming up is going up, there ain't no higher ground
So fuck it and let's get it on while the world's still turnin round!
*(Repeat the refrain a couple times, applause and obscenities for the singers.
Of the three, one girl of fifteen also serves as moderator, announcer.*

BRAT: Ladies and gentlemen . . . and everyone in between — wouldn't want
to leave anyone out!

(Laughter.)

The moment we've all been waiting for is about to begin — our great
show of rock wannabe's!

(Applause and enthusiasm. Girl continues.)

(Gross sounds.)

BRAT: Put a cork in it . . . or up it!

(More laughter and applause. The girl becomes serious.)

BRAT: Tonight, we are blessed with the presence of a much beloved man . . .
well . . . artist anyway *(Laughter.)* who has taken a long and arduous trip
. . . on LSD *(More laughter.)* just to be with us tonight. Applause for our
very own David Bowie!!

(Applause. A young David Bowie imitator stands up and receives the applause.)

BRAT: We also have with us — Brown Sugar — the most prodigious ass on
television . . . and she sings! Through her ass of course!

*(A young black girl dressed in a costume that accentuates her ass, stands up
and greets her fans, sticking her tongue out for which she receives a dozen
suggestive remarks.)*

BRAT: Let's begin with a little gift for the weaker sex . . . and also for the gals!
(Laughter.) What I mean is our own prince of the night — Macho! Au-
unuuu!

*(A young man dressed in black leather and earrings comes to the stage, he
gropes Brat who appears to enjoy it. H appears still dressed in his street cleaner
uniform and still under the effects of the drugs. He looks around, surprised,
not quite knowing what to do. He takes a wig off one person and puts it on
his head. Then he stands near some young people and tries to act like them.)*

H: Groovy, Huh?

*(The young people look at him as if he just crawled out from under a rock.
Without saying a word, they turn back to the show. The street cleaner continues and hums the code melody. The teenagers move away. H moves to another group.)*

H: For he's a jolly good fellow . . . for he's a jolly good fellow . . .

*(The teenagers hurriedly move away. Brat walks by and sees H's orange uni-
form. She's fascinated.)*

BRAT: Fabulous.

H: What?

BRAT: Your outfit. It's great!

H: Oh hey I'm looking for a young lady . . . *(He searches in his pocket for his instructions and finds them.)* Brat!

BRAT: That's me.

(She continues on her way. H stops her.)

H: Wait. I have to talk to you. It's very important.

BRAT: With me?

H: Yes. My life is in your hands!

BRAT: Write me!

(She leaves. H goes after her and takes her by the shoulders.)

H: You've got to listen to me!

BRAT: Look. I've got to change for my next scene — okay?

(H takes out the little plastic bags and shows them to her.)

H: Then what do I do with these? Return them?

(Brat looks at him in surprise, she stops a young man and whispers to him.)

BRAT: Ringo — tell Madonna that she should send in a substitute for me, just for tonight.

(The young man, very high, agrees with a strange head gesture and exits. The girl leads H through the door at the rear. Lights and sound turn background for the end of Macho's number. Applause. The young man thanks them and exits. Madonna enters and announces:)

MADONNA: And now — for all of you . . . Brown Sugar!

(The girl begins her striptease — with very little artistic talent and the sound and light fade as before. The general atmosphere, despite its youthful brashness, projects decadence.)

(In the bathroom, Brat has taken off part of her costume. She looks more and more like a child. She's furious. She turns on the water and takes out a metal box.)

BRAT: What's taken you so long? I've been crazy for a week!

H: I don't know. I'm new. This is my first delivery.

BRAT: Not only do they keep raising the price, but now they decide to deliver it whenever they fucking feel like it!

H: *(Looking at her.)* How old are you?

BRAT: What do you care! Where is it?

(H gives her the little bag. She opens it nervously. She puts some of the powder in a spoon and holds a lighter underneath. H is coming to. He watches her, fascinated.)

BRAT: Are you still here? Fuck off!

H: *(As if awakening.)* I have to speak to you . . . really I'm only here by accident. I'm accused of a crime I didn't commit. But I have to discover what crime I'm accused of in order to defend myself . . . that's why I accepted this commission. *(The girl has liquified the powder and is tying a strap around her arm.)* Your aunt is the one who is bringing charges against me . . . if you could speak to her, ask her what I did, maybe I could clear myself, defend myself . . . what are you doing?

(Brat has filled a syringe with an enormous needle. She is ready to plunge it into her arm, which is already covered with needle tracks. H reacts.)

H: No! No, don't do that! *(He stops her hand.)*

BRAT: What's your problem? Are you nuts?

(H grabs the syringe and smashes it on the floor. He then takes the metal box and empties the powder out. The girl tries to get it away from him. They struggle. Brat's reactions are increasingly infantile. She screams, she hits him and scratches him.)

H: I won't be part of this! No. No.

(He pushes her aside, breaks open the plastic bags and throws them in the toilet and flushes it. Brat howls. She puts her hands in the water trying to recuperate the powder, but it's hopeless.)

BRAT: Asshole! Asshole!

(She cries like a baby.)

(Blackout.)

Scene Four: The Comfort of Religion

In a corner of a cathedral, kneeling in front of a statue of the martyred Christ, H attempts to find relief from his pain.

H: God, why are you punishing me this way? I understand that I'm not the best of your children, but I'm not a jerk either . . . You know how much I'm suffering. Take pity on me, I beg you, enlighten me, tell me what I should do?

CHRIST: Ay my son, I really don't know. This country of yours has gotten completely out of hand.

(H is paralyzed. He looks incredulously at the sacred figure. Little by little, almost stumbling, he takes a few steps back. Just before he reaches the door, he runs out abandoning the holy shrine.)

(Blackout.)

Scene Five: A Dangerous Decision

A seedy hotel for poor transients. The flickering red neon sign with its name hardly illuminates the interior of a grimy, decrepit room. The door opens and H enters sweating and nervous. He goes to the sink and sticks his head under a thin stream of warm water that does succeed in refreshing him a bit. He takes a greyish cloth that hangs on the wall, wets it and covers his hair. He sits on the bed and lights a cigarette and smokes.

Outside we hear the sound of cars going by or parking in the bus terminal; a drunken whore; someone being mugged; and an organ grinder who is playing popular music off-key.

After calming himself down a little, he begins to empty his pockets. He takes off his uniform and hides the drugs in it. He folds the uniform carefully and takes it over to the window. He makes sure that no one is around and throws it in the garbage can. He closes the window and goes to the bed and lies down.

The man in the black raincoat goes to the garbage can and searches through it until he finds the drugs. He peeks in H's window and then exits.

H tries to sleep. He feels something walking on this body and he slaps it. The little feet continue their run. He slaps himself again and then two more times. He tries to get comfortable. But not for long. The tickling starts to spread. Alarmed. He lights a match and lifts the sheets.

H: Bed Bugs!

(He jumps out of bed and shakes himself. He doesn't know what to do. He lights a cigarette. He goes towards the window to analyze what chances he has on the street. He goes back to bed. He takes the sheet and shakes it. He rolls himself in it and goes to sit in a wooden chair where he remains balancing himself precariously until morning.)
(Blackout.)

Scene Six: At His Old Office

An environment of office machines and telephones that are constantly ringing. H finds himself in the reception area of a modern office, waiting to be noticed by a secretary busy with a talkative client. After a long wait, the young woman smiles at H. When she speaks, her voice sounds like she's swallowed an answering machine tape.

SECRETARY: And what can I do for you on this marvelous day?

H: I would like to speak with your boss.

SECRETARY: Do you have an appointment?

H: No.

SECRETARY: I'm sorry. He only sees people by appointment. Have a good day.

H: Miss, I've tried for three days now to make an appointment by phone, but he's always busy. I decided to drop by and see him personally.

SECRETARY: I'm sorry, but he only sees people by appointment. Have a good day.

H: Would you give him my card?

SECRETARY: I'm sorry. He's in a meeting and can't be disturbed. Have a good day.

H: Then I'm just going to sit here and wait until he comes out!

SECRETARY: No . . . no you can't.

H: Who said?

SECRETARY: *(Thinks for a moment.)* I don't remember. But it's not allowed.
(H goes and sits down. The secretary, vexed, watches him out of the corner of her eye.)

SECRETARY: He'll be a long time!

H: I don't care.

SECRETARY: Besides, he doesn't go out this way.

H: Well unless he flies out the window, he has to come out this way. You see, I used to work here. I know this place well.

SECRETARY: *(Intrigued.)* What's your name?

H: You have my card. Why don't you look at it?
(The secretary looks at it and is surprised. She looks at H, stands up and leaves. He entertains himself with a notebook. Something doesn't feel right. He turns and glimpses a door being quickly shut. This happens again and H realizes that the other employees are spying on him and giggling. H protests.)

H: Why don't you just come out and say hello?
(The door closes. A woman with a pail and a mop crosses. It is Faith, his old secretary. The woman sees him and her face lights up.)

FAITH: Sir. Sir. It's so good to see you! *(She embraces him.)* What are you doing here?

H: I came to get my things. And all this? *(Indicating the pail.)*

FAITH: *(Ashamed.)* This is the work I have now.

H: But a secretary as efficient as you?

FAITH: Ever since you left, I've been assigned to maintenance.
(The woman throws her mop against a door.)

FAITH: Go gossip yourselves to death! They couldn't fire me and I didn't want to quit, because of my pension — I only have three years left. They fired everyone else . . . I mean the employees who didn't officially give depositions against you.

H: That's ridiculous! Really, I've got to see the Licenciado, but they won't let me in to see him.

FAITH: He doesn't let anyone in. He loves having an office full of people waiting to see him. He invents very important meetings or calls from Ministers so that he doesn't have to see anyone. So the waiting room is always full. It makes him feel powerful, almost presidential.

H: I'd like his authorization to go over the documents that we handled when I was director, especially anything to do with the budget and administration. I want to make sure the numbers haven't been tampered with. *(Discretely.)* Could you help me?

FAITH: Ay, sir. There's nothing I'd love more, but nothing's here or anywhere I think.

H: What do you mean?

FAITH: I saw them myself. They were taking the drawers and files apart — dismantling everything. According to him, it was all going to the general archives, but from the way they were stuffing everything into plastic bags, there's no way it wasn't all thrown in the garbage.

H: Even our technical studies?

FAITH: Everything!

H: But that was valuable. It took years of work!

(The secretary enters and is annoyed to see them talking.)

SECRETARY: *(To Faith.)* May I ask what you are doing here?

FAITH: I'm going. I'm going. It was so good to see you, sir.

SECRETARY: Report to me before you leave work.

(Faith sticks out her tongue and exits. The secretary turns to H.)

SECRETARY: The Licenciado sends you his best wishes and asks you to excuse him for not being able to deal with you personally, but one of the Ministers called him on the red phone about a very important matter that requires his immediate attention.

(Two employees enter carrying a huge cardboard box.)

SECRETARY: Your personal belongings are in this box. We ask you to go through them thoroughly before you leave the building.

(H takes a look at it and with difficulty drags it along. The secretary follows him.)

SECRETARY: Please leave us your address and telephone number. But don't call us. We'll call you.

(*H turns to her and gives her the finger.*)

H: That's for you and your boss.

(*He exits with his box.*)

(*Blackout.*)

Scene Seven: The Wanderings

We see H wandering about different parts of the city, with no fixed destination, dragging his heavy cargo.
Blackness.

Scene Eight: The Nurse

H is having a sandwich on a park bench. His box is at his side. The man in the black raincoat is lurking nearby, hidden along the path. A young and pretty nurse enters. She sees H and sits down on the bench next to him.

H is deep in thought and hardly notices her. To get his attention, the nurse begins to sing. H looks at her out of the corner of his eye. The girl finishes singing and smiles. H smiles back. After making sure that no one is watching her, the nurse opens her blouse and shows him a breast. H looks at her, stupefied. She stays that way waiting for his comment. H finally understands what she wants and nods to her that she has a very nice breast. The nurse smiles, satisfied, and she tucks it away. She comes over and sits next to him. H becomes very nervous.

THE NURSE: You really like it?

H: Of course, you have a very pretty . . . they're very pretty!

THE NURSE: I do push ups every morning to keep them high and firm.

H: Oh really?

THE NURSE: It's the first thing that sags on a woman, especially if they're big.

H: I see.

THE NURSE: I also do exercises for my hips. Shall I show you?

H: No. I don't think that's necessary.

(*After a nervous pause, the nurse decides to go right to the point.*)

THE NURSE: So . . . lets go?

H: Where?

THE NURSE: *(Suggestively.)* Don't you want to see the rest?

H: Well yes of course that would be very interesting . . . but, why?

THE NURSE: You mean you don't get it? I'm a whore!

H: Huh? I thought you were a nurse.

THE NURSE: I am a nurse, but since I don't quite make enough to cover my expenses, I give myself a little help.

(She laughs contagiously. H ends up laughing too.)

THE NURSE: I don't know why — but men get excited by the idea of sleeping with a nurse.

H: Maybe they think that if you're a nurse here's no danger of contracting . . . *(He stops himself.)* Well you never know nowadays . . . the diseases.

THE NURSE: I know . . . and if I dress this way, it also keeps the police from bothering me.

H: Yes. Certainly!

THE NURSE: In fact, they take care of me.

(The two continue laughing. Finally the nurse becomes serious and stands up.)

THE NURSE: I live nearby. We can walk there.

H: Look, really, I'm sorry, but this time I'll have to pass on your very attractive invitation.

THE NURSE: *(Loses confidence.)* Why not? We'd have a good time.

H: I'm sure we would. And truly, you don't know how sorry I am, it's just that, I'm carrying this box around . . . and . . . I don't have much money.

THE NURSE: *(Quietly.)* I don't charge much money . . . all right?

(The nurse's friendliness has awakened in H a feeling of tenderness he has buried for a long time. The woman realizes this and smiles. She takes his hand. H still has doubts and looks at his box. She smiles.)

THE NURSE: Come on, I can help you with your box.

H: What the hell, let's go! Let the money be spent, let the world end . . . why prolong this agony!

(The girl doesn't understand H's words but continues smiling. They both carry the heavy box and walk away.)

(The man in the black rain coat comes out from behind a tree followed by another man in a black rain coat. They both walk behind the couple.)

(Blackout.)

Scene Nine: The Female Executive

A modern, well-equipped kitchen.

An army of servants is preparing a meal while the Señora, in her robe and slippers, directs them with great efficiency. She tries the soup with a long-handled spoon while the cook waits in anxious anticipation.

THE SEÑORA: It's not bad, but it needs a little more thyme.

(The cook is relieved and sighs. The Señora continues her inspection. She tries a stew and again we see everyone tense up and then relax when she smiles.)

THE SEÑORA: Not bad, but don't add the white wine and the sherry together. You add the sherry as it's being served.

(She sees two servant girls preparing a garlic dish and rushes over.)

THE SEÑORA: No, noo — if you add the oil like that it'll curdle. Ay, what a girl — don't you have an ounce of common sense? Let me do it. You keep beating the egg yolks without stopping. Look, the oil should be poured like this, like a little thread . . . you see? All right, you can continue.

(A servant boy enters with the phone.)

BOY: Señora, your office.

THE SEÑORA: Again! Shit. Can't they leave me alone for a moment. I can't get anything done!

(In a bad mood, she takes the phone.)

THE SEÑORA: Doctor, I told you not to forward any calls. I told you I have to prepare this party for Quique . . . what? All right, tell me . . . just what are these very important calls?

(She sits down crossly with the phone in her lap.)

THE SEÑORA: What . . . The Soviet embassy? The ambassador? Well tell him I'm extremely busy. You take care of him. You know about all that stuff anyway. Yes, and what else? I see . . . A cultural exchange with Afghanistan? Jesus, what do I care about Afghanistan? I don't even know where it is! Well, hand that over to my astrologer — he was the one who came up with the idea.

(The pastry chef has approached and is trying to signal her.)

THE SEÑORA: What did you say?

PASTRY CHEF: Is this enough butter?

THE SEÑORA: What do you mean butter! You should be using "creme fraiche" . . . this isn't a cake from Denny's. *(Into the phone.)* One moment doctor, it's that the help here is . . .

(She puts the phone down and faces the pastry chef who begins to tremble as if she had Saint Vitus disease.)

THE SEÑORA: All right. Do I have to do everything myself? Why did you think I took out the tray of creme fraiche?

PASTRY CHEF: Forgive me, Señora, I beg you . . .

THE SEÑORA: Last time it was the cocoa . . . frankly, I don't think you're capable of making a decent cake for my nephew!

PASTRY CHEF: I'll be more careful . . .

THE SEÑORA: And creme fraiche! Use creme fraiche! I want my little Quique to eat a cake just like his grandmother used to make . . . and if it doesn't come out this time, just wait and see what happens to all of you!

(Terror in the kitchen. Plates fall, fingers are cut. Frightened faces all around, while the woman, oblivious, continues her telephone conversation.)

THE SEÑORA: Excuse me doctor, but we almost had a catastrophe here . . . so . . . what? I've got the upper hand now. All right, now what were you saying? The budget? Well I won't lie to you, I haven't looked it over yet — it's just that it's very long! Look, tell the colonel that I okay it just as it is, I trust his good judgment. *(Hangs up and says to herself.)* I mean really how much do I know about the schedule or the budget?

(The chef approaches her cautiously and holds out a dish for her to taste. She approves it. The phone rings again. The woman exchanges a gesture of impatience with the chef.)

THE SEÑORA: Now what? . . . what? What's burning? Well call the firemen, not me — What, do you want me to go there with a bucket and throw water on it? *(Comments to the chef.)* Jesus what incompetents! Is that all? What? A meeting with the minister? No, no tell him straight out that I can't. It's my little Quique's birthday that's why! . . . what? Why can't you tell him that? Okay, all right, tell him something else. Whatever . . . yeah that's good, that's a good one. Yes and have Enriquez go in my place.

(Mortal silence on the other end of the phone.)

THE SEÑORA: Well, doctor . . . doctor are you there? Didn't you hear me? Yes, that's just what I said, that Enriquez go in my place. What — he's in jail? You must be kidding! What did he do? I did? When? No you must be wrong — no that would be the colonel when I went to Egypt. No I would never do that, he's a very serious and decent man. Besides he's a Scorpio. Ay. Don't tell me . . . *(She bursts out laughing.)* Poor Enriquez, what a shame. No you must have misunderstood me. Of course, reinstate him immediately! What do you mean how? Simple, fire the Licenciado who's there and be done with it! Enriquez has more of a right to it, he came

on board first. Besides, he's a Scorpio. You know what that means. The
other was a Sagittarius. Yes, please, you handle this personally.

(She hangs up and remains thoughtful.)

THE WOMAN: Ay, I don't why they made me cultural director in the first place
. . . I really don't.

*(A great rush of police, telephones, loudspeakers mobilize immediately look-
ing for H, breaking up the stillness of the night.)*

(Blackout.)

SCENE TEN: A Man Without a Future

*A loft in a small stone building. H and the nurse have just made love and
remain entwined on the bed, exhausted. For the first time in a long time H
feels relaxed and at peace, one could almost say happy. Without disturbing their
pleasant closeness, they begin to talk. A light conversation, saying what he already knows to be true, but adding to it the pleasure of this confirmation.*

H: I didn't think I could do it.

NURSE: Could do what?

H: I thought I'd never be able to make love again.

NURSE: Mmmmmm.

H: My wife's favorite joke was to call me her Christmas tree. She said that everything that hung from me was an ornament.

(The nurse smiles. She kisses his shoulder. She adds quietly.)

NURSE: I can't complain.

H: Do you know, I came with you — more than anything — because I didn't
have anywhere to leave my box?

NURSE: You devil!

(They play around lovingly.)

What about your house?

H: I don't have one. I lost it along the way. When I met you, I was trying to
figure out what I would do with my life, including, doing away with myself. Of course, I wouldn't have dared, I was too afraid. That's something
I don't understand. I'm afraid of death when life seems empty, and now
that I feel more alive, I feel like I'm less afraid to face it.

NURSE: Don't face it. Let's enjoy life together.

H: That's a decision I can't make anymore.

NURSE: Why not?

H: My time on bail is about to end and I won't let them put me in jail again — at least not as long as I'm alive. Also there's some drug dealers after me. I ruined their business. They've got to be looking for me now. On top of that, I've seen some guy in a black raincoat who seems to be following me . . . so you can see I'm a man without a future.

NURSE: So never leave and they'll never find you! I'll take care of you, I'll feed you and we'll make love all the time.

H: I wish I could do that, but I've got to go now — maybe the sooner the better.

NURSE: No!

H: I don't want to involve you in my life at this point. I'd be putting your life in danger too.

NURSE: So? If I'm alone nothing matters! With you, I feel so alive, I want to keep what we have.

H: We don't have anything. And if something were to happen to you, I'd never forgive myself.

NURSE: The worst that could happen would be that you leave. Stay here with me, at least for tonight. Hold me close and make me dream that this is the best of worlds, that we can still find happiness and that you'll always love me and take care of me like this for the rest of our lives.

(They embrace and kiss and make love again. The light fades. Some hours later there's an insistent noise, like rats gnawing. H wakes up. He sits up in bed and listens. Those aren't rats. There's something metallic in the sound. What it really sounds like is someone fiddling with the lock. Alarmed, he turns on the light.)

NURSE: *(Awakening.)* What's going on? What is it?

H: Sssshhhhhhh. Someone's playing with the lock!

(They watch the doorknob turning.)

H: What should I do?

NURSE: Throw something at them.

H: Why . . . what for?

NURSE: It might scare them away.

(H takes a shoe and throws it against the door. The noise stops. A long pause. Nothing happens. The lovers wait expectantly. The nurse goes to the door and puts her ear to it. She listens for a moment and returns to bed.)

NURSE: I don't hear anyone. I bet they've left.

H: Do you know who it could be?

NURSE: No. Some drunk maybe . . . someone who had the wrong floor.

(The hypothesis doesn't seem very convincing. The lovers remain upset. H

smokes. The nurse hugs him to calm him. All of a sudden a violent kick throws the door open against the wall. The Chief and his subordinate enter. H pales.)

H: You again? And now what?

(There's no answer. The men slowly advance towards them.)

(Blackout.)

SCENE ELEVEN: Nothing Happened Here

H's office just after dawn. H arrives with his box and puts it in the middle of his office. He looks around and then begins the sad task of putting his things back where they were. Loud footsteps get his attention. It's the Señora accompanied by the Subordinate. The Chief.

THE SEÑORA: Ay, you don't know how sorry I am, but that's the way things go in government. The good news is that it's all over and you're free of guilt. Here's your office, your job and your budget — so get on with it — nothing's really happened.

(The Professor appears.)

PROFESSOR: With us, you'll have the opportunity to change all this shit, at least to try . . . at least to try . . . at least to try.

(H smiles at him and continues unpacking his box. At the back the light comes up on the nurse.)

NURSE: Let's get out of here. Let's start over in some other place . . . in some other place.

(H stops what he's doing and goes to her, full of emotion. He's about to caress her face when the men in the black raincoats appear and stand behind her. H retreats fearfully. His wife and son enter.)

WIFE: You don't know how happy I was when I read the news. I immediately packed my things and came back to be at your side, as always, in the best of times.

(She pulls the boy.)

WIFE: Go on! Go give your father a hug. *(To H.)* He's missed you so much . . . go ahead!

(The boy, crying, locks himself around his mother's leg. H finishes putting his things away. Then he begins to take his clothes off. With great care he hangs everything on a wooden hanger.)

(Faith appears.)

FAITH: From the way they stuffed everything in plastic bags, I'd say all our work was thrown in the garbage.

(Big Shot also appears.)

BIG SHOT: But — hey, why are you so discouraged? Politics is like that; we're always beginning.

(The Capo appears.)

CAPO: You're in a big mess, but we can get you out of it.

(And the mother.)

MOTHER: Remember, everything I did, I did for your well-being.

(H has finished undressing. He sets everything on fire. His memories, like silent spectators, watch as H gets in his box and closes the top. The light fades, we hear a gunshot.)

END OF PLAY

MEXICO, USA
A Murder Mystery in Two Acts

IN REGARD TO MY WORK

This play should really be called *Mexico, MO.,* but very few people in Mexico would have understood the abbreviation. They probably would have thought I meant Mexico, Morelos. It was with this piece that I began my artistic activities at my Dramatic Arts Center (CADEE), whose initials should be CAD. However, when I went to register the name I found that all the possible combinations of those letters were taken. I had to change the name to Center for Dramatic Arts and Specialized Studies for the Stage. Which was the shortest version I could find that worked.

At that time, a Cultural Decentralization Program had given me a grant ($100,000) to open my core school with the condition that I locate it in the provinces. I chose Cuernavaca because of its proximity to Mexico City (60 kms) and because it was the only city outside of Mexico City with a large number of artists, intellectuals and scientists (even though the latter are like ghosts one only sees at the market), and most importantly because it is close to Ocotepec (3 kms), the village where I have lived since 1980.

Grant in hand, I went to see the governor to ask for a building where I could set up both my school and a theater and to request an additional grant for operating expenses. I got lucky. The governor was one of the few cultured politicians in the country, plus he was acquainted with my work and felt honored that I had chosen his State as the site for my theater. Two weeks later, he had already found me a beautiful theater in the downtown area (previously a porno house) and a five-year grant similar to the one I'd already received. I immediately bought used equipment (lights, consoles, apparatus, etc.) through friends in New York, and I converted the 2000-seat porno house into an acting school with two theaters; one with 400 seats and the other with 100. The rest of the building served as classrooms, workshops, storage , etc.

My problems began when I attempted to open the school. It seemed that in this city of close to a million people, home of artists, intellectuals, and scientists, no one enrolled in the classes — despite the fabulous group of teachers I managed to bring together and despite the fact that I was in my "prime" (the most award-winning playwright in the Mexican theater). And it wasn't that no one was interested in theatre — almost one half of the population wanted to be actors. What they didn't want was to study to be actors.

I changed my strategy. Instead of trying to enroll people in classes, I solicited actors to produce *Mexico, USA*. In one week I found myself with over 100 people wanting to audition. I chose 50 of the best of the worst, and after showing them their inability to get up on stage — their voices being inaudible, their complete lack of any understanding of even one theatrical work —

I made them go to class as a condition of hiring them as a part of the cast. (The majority studied as actors and the rest stayed on as stage managers, lighting technicians, etc.) These were the students I opened the school with. Three weeks later, in January 1990, we began rehearsals for *Mexico, USA.*

Our unexpected critical and popular success (three national prizes) cured the student problem. Every year after that, our subscriptions and the prestige of the school grew. (The artists, intellectuals, and scientists never did arrive).

Our curriculum and theater repertory were guided by this experience.We decided that fifty students a year would be the maximum with four semesters of classes. We would incorporate the most advanced students, the best in their classes, in each production. New arrivals would have to audition. The criteria for planning the season was to pick works that would use the greatest number of students. We had quickly learned that the students learned much more quickly on stage than in the classroom. We did Miller's *View From The Bridge* with thirty-seven actors. (It was written for fifteen). Each student who worked in a production either as an actor or as a technician earned a very modest salary which allowed us to cover some of their expenses and gave them a kind of professional status that inspired them. Graduates earned more than the advanced students who in turn earned more than the beginners. Almost all of our students earned more than their enrollment fees. This system allowed us to keep costs down while producing sizable plays that were costly to stage. In two years we had a tremendous cast of actors and technicians that worked with us enthusiastically and happily for over five years until our cultured governor was replaced by one who lacked visible culture. This governor's first public act — eight days after taking over the governorship — was to close our school very peremptorily as if we were a bordello or a bar. . . .

TO END WITH AN ANECDOTE . . .

The pretext for the closure was an eight month audit during which we were not allowed to enter the school — even to retrieve personal belongings. Students and teachers staged constant protests, but no one paid the least attention (Long Live the Powerful!). Eight months later, a casual article in the newspaper stated that the audit had found no misuse of funds. By then the damage had been done. The school was lost. We never knew what really happened since there was never an official explanation. But keeping things under wraps only encouraged gossip. Soon the most imaginative scenarios were in circulation concerning the closure of the school. It was said that the governor and the head of the school were after the same woman . . . that the governor decided to trash the school because it was subversive and anti-government. I have my own version. During his short term in office (three out of a five-year term) Cuernavaca became one of the most violent cities in the country and a refuge for the most conspicuous, reputed drug traffickers ("The King of the Skies" is mentioned in the movie *Traffic*). Therefore, how could this Governor let the author of *Mexico USA* run an acting conservatory exactly across from the Governor's Palace?

CHARACTERS

Nick Gomez
Ruth Gordon
Helen Esparza
Rosa de Guadalajara
Diana Rand
Al Gallegos
Carlos Gonzalez
Tiro Labrador de Yecapixtla
Military Officer
Ronald Reagan
Jack Colby
Sergeant O'Hara
Bill
Young Officer
Old Lady
Commissioner Welles
Motel Receptionist
Janet Falco
Television Announcer
Drunk Driver
Alvy Gallegos
Oliver North
Columbian Drug Dealer Roberto Suarez
Colombian Minister Lara Bonilla
W. Casey
Ramon "The Cuban"
Lee Hamilton
Louis
Tim
Becky

Collie

"El Mexicano"

Customers at Nick's cafe, street people, nurses, reporters, photographers, United Nations representatives, women in mourning, pushers, military personnel, etc.

The action takes place at the end of the 80s. The central plot is fictional; the surroundings, speeches and statistics are real. Some of these facts are presented on screen.

Mexico, USA opened at the Ocampo Theater in Cuernavaca, Mexico in 1990 and won the following awards from the Mexican Association of Theater Critics: Best Play of theYear, Best Production of the Year, and Best Regional Company.

ACT ONE

A police station in Mexico County, Missouri. In one of the basement rooms, four individuals of Mexican descent are being interrogated by the local authorities.

The first is a man of about forty, prematurely aged. His white hair contrasts with his clay-colored face, a result of constant exposure to the sun and dust; it gives him a slightly saturnine aspect.

White light comes on, bathing only his face. The man is startled. He looks around him moving only his eyes. Suddenly, in the dark, a blackboard with red letters lights up in front of him and an electronic interrogation begins.

BLACKBOARD: Name

(The man observes the words that are also reflected on his face and understands that he is being questioned. Not knowing whom to address, he talks to the blackboard. However, his attitude clearly shows that this questioning has become routine.)

NICK: Oh! My name is Nicanor, Nicanor Gomez — but everybody calls me "Nick." I'm forty-two years old, married and have children. All of them born here except Maria, the oldest, who was born in Morelia.

BOARD: Citizenship.

NICK: Mexican by birth, but I've been an American citizen for twenty years.

BOARD: Sex.

NICK: Heyyy . . . what do you think! *(He tries to laugh, but he's too nervous.)*

BOARD: Occupation.

NICK: I own a coffee shop. I opened it five years ago — when my mother, "la jefa," died you know, then I didn't need to send my pesos to the other side. So, I saved my pennies and stayed in the States. Before that I worked in the fields picking grapes, some cotton . . .

(A sharp annoying buzzer sounds a few times, as if it's some prehistoric bird.)

BOARD: Just answer the questions.

(The man looks at the board, surprised.)

NICK: Yes sir . . . or lady!

BOARD: Religion.

NICK: Catholic. We're all Catholic in my home . . . which is your home too, of course.

BOARD: What?

NICK: We're all Catholic in my home.

BOARD: Have you ever been to Cuba or Nicaragua?

NICK: *(Alarmed.)* Me? No, senor, God forbid. I've only been in Michoacan and from Michoacan to here . . . and since la jefa died . . . not even there anymore.

BOARD: Have you ever been involved in political activities?

NICK: *(In terror.)* No, no, never, I swear I was never a communist!

(He crosses himself with his fingers and kisses them. However, the board buzzes as a name and date appear.)

BOARD: Delano, California 1968

(Nick knows what this means.)

NICK: Jesus — but that was years ago . . . and it wasn't even a political movement, never communist. We staged a protest because they wanted to pay us less. Because some of the guys were wetbacks and couldn't complain. And besides they wanted to charge us for lodging — can you believe that?

(He's disconcerted because he doesn't know who to direct his remarks to.)

NICK: Some stinking chicken coop where they had us all piled on top of each other . . .

BOARD: Have you ever tried drugs?

NICK: *(Continuing from before.)* All we got out of it was being fired. Since then you can bet I've never protested anything, not even a mosquito bite.

(A buzzer interrupts him. Nick looks at the board.)

BOARD: Have you ever tried drugs?

NICK: Oh! Sorry . . . drugs? No. Never!

BOARD: Any members of your family?

NICK: Don't even think about it. In my family, we never do shit like that!

BOARD: Do you know Ruth Gordon?

NICK: Who?

BOARD: Ruth Gordon!

(A roadside motel, a couple is laughing and playing around in the hallway. The woman is thirty-five, slender and attractive, almost beautiful. The man is tall, well built. He wears a poncho, a Mexican sombrero and has a full dark mustache. The man opens one of the doors, takes the woman in his arms and walks into the room humming the wedding march. Through the window, in the half-light, we see that the man carries her directly to the bed and without preliminaries tries to have sex with her. The woman resists a little. It appears that she proposes something to him. The man stands up, he takes off the poncho, the sombrero and puts them to one side. Afterwards he takes a small briefcase and goes into the bathroom. When the lights go on, the man's shadow looms large and his actions are blurry. The woman gets out of bed lightly and goes to the window, closing the curtains behind her. She stands

there a moment, squinting into the darkness. She nervously lights a cigarette and continues moving the flame from the lighter from one side to the other, her face worried. Suddenly, someone turns car lights on and off — like a ghostly code. The woman seems to calm down.

Light, Nick observes the young woman as if he's seeing a photograph.)

NICK: That's Ruth Gordon? Yeah, I know her. She's been coming to the cafe for some time now. Pretty often, really good-looking, that woman, very friendly . . . Just a few guys in the cafe have a crush on her!

BOARD: Did you have a sexual affair with her?

NICK: Me? With her? Don't I wish! No, those kind of fleas don't jump on my bed.

BOARD: The answer isn't clear.

NICK: What I mean is . . . I'm married and my wife don't give me permission to have affairs with no one, okay?

(In the bungalow, the man opens the curtain, surprising her. He appears to question her. She shows him her cigarette. This seems to quell his doubts. The man takes a small mirror with two lines of white powder and inhales one of the lines through a straw. He then passes it to the young lady who inhales the other line. The amorous games begin again. The woman lets him caress her for a moment, then pulls herself away and goes to the bathroom. The man follows her. Through the textured glass, we see the man push her into the shower even though she's dressed. The figures disappear.)

(The interrogation continues.)

BOARD: When was the last time you saw her?

NICK: The last I saw her was . . . let me see . . . the day before yesterday, in the evening. She stayed for about an hour and only drank one cup of coffee. She looked really nervous. Finally, el bato came and took her away.

BOARD: Who?

NICK: Some guy who looked like Jorge Negrete . . . with his charro hat. We'd never seen him at the cafe before.

BOARD: Describe him in more detail.

NICK: I can't really . . . I didn't see him that well, you know. He didn't come in . . . he tapped on the window from the outside. She went out right away. They got into a SUV and they left.

BOARD: Whose SUV?

NICK: Hers, I suppose. She always drove around in a red SUV.

(The lights fade on his face. In the bathroom the amorous playfulness becomes violently sexual. The man grabs the woman out of the shower, strips her and makes her act out his fantasies, finally having sex with her almost like an an-

imal. The woman throws herself to the ground in a desperate attempt to get away from his painful advances. The man goes after her and their figures disappear behind the macabre glass.)

(The lights go up on the next detained person. It's a man of fifty-five, dressed as a Shriner who tries to be charming but his smile seems more like a grimace.)

AL: My name is Al Galigous, American citizen and very proud of it!

(A shrill buzz and a red light illuminates his face.)

BOARD: That's not your name!

AL: What are you talking about? . . . oh, I get it. It's that, that's the way you people pronounce it. My real name is Alvaro Gallegos. I was born in Mexico, but I've been a citizen here for fifteen years. And fifteen years ago my country was veering off towards communism, so I packed up my things and moved up here for good. I'm fifty-five years old, married and I've been a great admirer of this free and democratic country ever since I was allowed to complete my graduate studies in Boston.

(Buzz.)

BOARD: Just answer the questions.

AL: Oh yes, of course. Sorry.

BOARD: Occupation?

AL: I'm a chemical engineer. I graduated with the highest grades of any foreigner . . . *(Buzz.)* . . . okay, okay . . . I now work as a sales rep. for Ayerts Laboratories.

BOARD: Religion?

AL: Catholic, of course.

BOARD: Have you ever been to Cuba or Nicaragua?

AL: Of course not. I voted for Reagan.

BOARD: Have you ever been involved in political activities?

AL: Never.

BOARD: Religious associations.

AL: Well . . . no

(Buzz.)

BOARD: KKK, 1973!

AL: Well yes . . . but I only went once. It was a big mistake. I never went again.

BOARD: Have you ever tried drugs?

AL: Never!

BOARD: Have any of your family tried drugs?

AL: Definitely not!

(Buzzing and red light. Al is disconcerted.)

BOARD: Wrong answer

AL: What do you mean, "wrong answer"? I swear on my mother's grave . . .
(The buzzing and red light continue . . . Al gets angry.)

AL: Oh no! No, no, no. You're the ones that're wrong here. I would know, believe me. You can't hide these things. I challenge anyone, anyone who says differently to show me, to prove it to me!

BOARD: Do you know Ruth Gordon?

AL: Throw that in too . . . eh? Ruth Gordon? Yes I met her. She came to our house a couple times. She was very interested in my son Alvy . . . a passing fancy. She was much older than my son.
(Buzzer.)

BOARD: Why did you say "was"?

AL: *(Nervous.)* Did I say that? I wasn't aware . . . I guess I used the past tense since it's been quite a while since we've heard anything about her. Why?
(The light on his face fades.)
(In the motel bathroom the light is turned off and the man comes out into the bedroom carrying the woman in his arms. She seems to be unconscious. He takes her to the bed and lays her down. Then he ties her hands and feet. He notices the window and closes the curtain.)
(The third person detained is an elegant and distinguished young man. He's furious about being held.)

CARLOS: My name is Carlos Gonzalez, Mexican and I came to this godforsaken town to buy some horses for a farm I own outside of Chicago. I'm an important official of the Mexican government . . . and that's all I'm going to say to you people until I talk to my lawyer.

BOARD: Have you ever been involved in political activities?
(Carlos ignores the board. He takes out a cigar from a fancy cigar case, lights it and begins to smoke despite the buzzing and red light flashing across his face. Finally he takes off a shoe and throws it at the board. He shouts.)

CARLOS: Turn off the damn light — it's bothering my eyes.
(The board makes a strange sound like a wounded dog and the light becomes weaker. However, the board keeps flashing.)

BOARD: Have you ever been involved in political activities?

CARLOS: Yes, from the day I was born. These days I'm a member of my country's official party where I've been a civil servant, a deputy, and . . .
(The buzzing interrupts him.)

BOARD: In the USA?

CARLOS: What? In the United States? No. I'd have to be really fucked to belong to a Party of gringos.

BOARD: Have you ever tried drugs?

CARLOS: I take Valium every day to sleep.

BOARD: Illegal drugs!

CARLOS: What a stupid question. No! And if I had tried them, I wouldn't say so!

BOARD: Have you ever been to Cuba or Nicaragua?

CARLOS: Of course I've been to those countries. They're friends of Mexico. I've also been to the Soviet Union, Angola and Vietnam. I'm a good friend of Castro and other leaders of the socialist block, the tenacious defender of the free auto determination of nations. And I think your President Reagan's policies towards Nicaragua are deplorable. So, is my international position clear?

BOARD: Are you an enemy of the United States?

CARLOS: No. But I'm your enemy for making me go through this ridiculous interrogation. But an enemy of the American people . . . of course not. What did those poor people do to deserve leaders who show TV bingo games in prison!?

BOARD: Do you have a criminal record in the United States?

CARLOS: No, but I will have if I get a hold of the asshole who ordered me detained!

BOARD: Do you know Ruth Gordon?

CARLOS: Ruth who?

BOARD: Ruth Gordon!

CARLOS: No.

(Buzzing and red lights.)

BOARD: The Mexican embassy, December the 12th

CARLOS: (Thinks for a moment.) A dark haired lady with a great ass? Yes, I know her. She practically assaulted me at that party. I think she was half crazy. First, she invites herself to my hotel, but once we were in my room, anything romantic stopped and she disappeared as soon as I went into the bathroom . . .

BOARD: Did you have drugs there?

CARLOS: Stop with the drugs! . . . although now I remember she kept after me . . . did you guys send her? She was after me every minute asking me to find her some good drugs. Finally joking, I told her that if she wanted to get high, we should go to Las Vegas . . .

BOARD: Why Las Vegas?

CARLOS: Cause there . . . in any hotel . . . they'll supply you with all the drugs you want.

BOARD: How do you know that?

CARLOS: Frank Sinatra movies! *(To himself.)* Assholes!

BOARD: Did you have drugs in Las Vegas?

CARLOS: *(Annoyed.)* We didn't go to Las Vegas, we didn't take drugs and that was the first and last time I ever saw Ruth Gordon!

(He gives the board the finger and turns away, ending the interview. The light fades from his face.)

(In the motel room, the curtain opens and we see the woman stumbling around. Weakly she lights her cigarette lighter and moves the flame from one side to the other. The car lights come on again, lighting up her face which is as battered and bloody as the rest of her. She clumsily tries to open the window. She can't. Some hands grab her by the throat and pull her back. The woman weakly tries to resist, but after a few seconds of struggle she disappears behind the curtain. The car lights go out and we hear a car engine starting up.)

(A lamp is lit near the fourth detained person, an Indian from Morelos who starts to talk in Nahuatl when he gets scared.)

TIRO: Nefa amo. Nefa nic negui ni mo guepas. Guei no tegui tu nefa axic aniguile amitla amiga. *(I'm innocent. I didn't do nothing to that lady! I've never hurt no one! I want to go back to Yecapixtla.)*

(Buzzing and red light.)

BOARD: Speak English!

TIRO: Uh?

BOARD: Habla Ingles!

TIRO: Huh?

(We hear a computerized voice.)

VOICE: Don't you understand English?

TIRO: Yes. But I can't read.

VOICE: What's your name?

TIRO: Tiro Labrador de Yecapixtla!

VOICE: And what are you doing up here?

TIRO: I left my town because there was nothing to eat. Two of my kids died last year from hunger . . . so, I said to myself, Tiro, it's time to look somewhere else, so I came to Laredo as a wetback. I've been working for a year at the hotel but I want to go home. As soon as I get enough money to buy a market stall back home, I'm leaving. Here it's freezing and, I tell you the truth, although there's food here, a hell of a lot of food, it all tastes terrible!

VOICE: That's enough. How did you know Ruth Gordon? .

TIRO: The woman in seventeen?

VOICE: Yes.

TIRO: Well . . . let me tell you . . . it would have been in the early morning when I heard sounds and I got up, thinking the people had checked out. *(He acts out the things he's telling.)* I went to the storage room to get some clean sheets and cleaning things . . .

(A man in military dress goes down the hallway.)

TIRO: *(With his laundry cart.)* Then I saw that the car, the car of those people in seventeen was pulling out . . .

VOICE: So early?

TIRO: That happens in a motel, you know. You'll excuse me for saying it — but most of the people just go there to fuck and then they leave . . . they even leave the lights on *(Smiles.)* and you get to see almost everything . . .

VOICE: That's enough. Stay with the story . . .

(The Indian has arrived at the room.)

TIRO: When I got to the room, I saw that the door was open and I went in . . . to do the cleaning . . .

(He goes into the room, turns on the light, opens the curtains and begins to clean. He picks up the towels that are thrown on the floor and takes them into the bathroom. There, he turns on the light and finds the naked, limp body of Ruth Gordon hanging.)

TIRO: Ay, my God . . . Oh my God!

(He's terrified.)

(On television, President Reagan is giving a speech:)

REAGAN: The communist government of Nicaragua poses an extraordinary threat to the safety of our country; therefore I am declaring a permanent state of emergency . . .

(The screen changes, Jack Colby, a news commentator, appears.)

JACK: Once again, President Reagan dwells on the communist menace — his major preoccupation in foreign affairs. The president asked Congress for more financial aid to support the armed struggle of the democratic forces, which are fighting communism in Nicaragua . . .

REAGAN: I'm sure that Congress will support my efforts to help these freedom fighters — our only barrier to Soviet domination in our region. The cause of liberty and our national security are intricately linked to those of Central America. This threat is too close to home to ignore . . .

JACK: However, Congress stood firm in refusing the requested aid; Instead they approved the Hughes Ryan Amendment to regulate clandestine operations by the White House. Congress also ratified the Boland Amendment, which prohibits any official agency involved in spying to assist Anti-Sandinista forces. Thus Congress has presented the president with his greatest defeat in his fight against Nicaraguan government since he took office.

JACK: For its part, the world court at the Hague rejected the accusation that Nicaragua was exporting its revolution to El Salvador and vetoed any intervention in that country.

REAGAN: I regret that my hands are tied, thus playing into the hands of communism. But I promise I won't remain passive while our neighbors in the Isthmus are being added to the list of nations held hostage by communism. Neither will I be tied to any decision the World Court has made concerning Nicaragua. And I will never permit the Sandinistas to win in direct defiance of our interests. Our moral values, our movements will only be secure in a democratic neighborhood.

JACK: Now for the local news . . .

(The image changes to a photograph of the motel room, emphasizing the body of Ruth Gordon. On the photo the words "Macabre Discovery.")

JACK: At the Motel Paisano Drive, the body of a young woman was discovered hanging from . . .

(A mannequin is hanging at the site instead of Ruth Gordon. Outside we see a crowd of curious onlookers, police, and journalists milling around. The news commentator is now inside the room.)

JACK: The motives for such a brutal crime are still unknown, but the bruises and other signs of violence on the cadaver seem to indicate it was a crime of passion.

(Sergeant O'Hara passes by with a brick of coke.)

O'HARA: Cocaine. Enough to kill a horse!

JACK: You heard it here — drugs, passion — a deadly combination.

(Tiro passes escorted by Bill, a young policeman.)
(Going towards them.)

JACK: This is the young janitor from the motel who discovered the body, and is one of the principal suspects. The police find it difficult to believe that he was working legitimately in the early morning hours when the crime took place . . . What do you have to say about this?

(He holds the microphone out to Tiro, who is frightened and begins to speak in Nahuatl.)

TIRO: Por inom onesh macaque, para ni teguitis. Nefa tiano a Tochan!

JACK: I didn't understand a word . . . Did you?

(The policeman shakes his head.)

JACK: *(To Tiro.)* What language were you speaking? Don't you speak English?

TIRO: Oh yes. It's that when I get nervous I talk in Nahuatl . . . I was just say-
ing I don't have a work schedule . . . I work all the time, any time I'm
needed. That was in the contract when they hired me . . .
*(An old lady breaks away from the crowd of onlookers and throws herself on
Tiro.)*
LITTLE OLD LADY: Murderer . . . Murderer!
*(She grabs him by the hair and throws him to the floor and scratches and
beats him. Jack comments on the scene.)*
JACK: An old lady, possibly a witness to the crime or perhaps a relative of the
victim, has violently attacked the janitor . . . She's obviously very angry
. . . You can observe how distraught she is.
(The police separate them. Jack goes up to her.)
JACK: You saw him murder the woman?
LITTLE OLD LADY: What?
JACK: Were you a witness at the crime scene?
LITTLE OLD LADY: No.
JACK: Are you a relative of the murder victim? *(To the camera.)*
I'm asking if she's related to the victim.
LITTLE OLD LADY: No.
JACK: Then why were you attacking him?
LITTLE OLD LADY: He's a Mexican, ain't he?
JACK: *(Turning towards the camera.)* Cut! Cut!
(The old lady moves away. Jack shows a woman's purse.)
JACK: A number of marijuana joints were found in the woman's purse. They
also discovered an appointment book with the names and addresses of
three Hispanic males, who apparently have, it seems already been detained.
Can you confirm that, officer?
O'HARA: *(To the camera.)* Mexicans have a biological disposition for crime. It's
a proven anthropological fact. They're usually the ones who commit the
worst atrocities around here, although, of course, we can't discount the
possibility that this could have been done by Negroes or Arabs.
JACK: The motel receptionist couldn't supply any significant information.
MOTEL RECEPTIONIST: It's that . . . I was watching an episode of *Dallas* . . .
right in that part where JR. found his wife with another man!
JACK: But didn't you see them when they registered?
MOTEL RECEPTIONIST: She was the one who paid. I only noticed that the guy
was wearing a very large sombrero and was whispering dirty things in her
ear in Spanish!
JACK: Oh, do you speak Spanish?

MOTEL RECEPTIONIST: No . . .

JACK: But then? CUT! Cut the video tape!

(A young woman appears, crying. Jack sees her and comments.)

JACK: Janet Falco, a student of American literature, was the first to identify her. What can you tell us about the woman?

JANET: Her name was Ruth Gordon. We were roommates. We shared an apartment . . .

(She can't speak and becomes hysterical. Commissioner Welles appears and with some briskness moves her away.)

JACK: *(Confused.)* Don't go away. We'll be right back with more coverage of this gruesome event.

(In the Oval Office, President Reagan and some of his associates.)

REAGAN: So this is how Congress has decided to prevent me from keeping my word to help the Nicaraguan Contras. Well, It's not an option. Gentlemen, I've called you here, my best men, my closest associates, to see how we get around Congress to obtain the necessary funds to continue this war. I understand it won't be easy. We'll have to get the money from other sources, perhaps clandestine sources . . .

(On screen: Operation Elephant. The president authorizes sending military surplus from the Pentagon to the Contras and the gathering of funds, outside of Congress, in a clandestine operation that will involve everyone including the Vatican.)

(Commissioner Welles' office. He enters with Janet Falco.)

WELLES: Sit here. You'll be more comfortable.

(He shows her to an old leather couch. The young woman sits down. Welles goes to his desk and takes out a file.)

WELLES: So tell me, Janet Falco, your relationship with the deceased was . . .

JANET: *(Still upset.)* We lived together.

WELLES: Do you know who killed her?

JANET: No!

WELLES: Someone you might suspect?

JANET: No one.

WELLES: Talk to me about her.

JANET: There's not much I can say . . . I've only known her a month. I put up an advertisement at the University for a roommate. We spoke. I liked her and we decided to share an apartment . . .

WELLES: What did she do in town?

JANET: She worked preparing tourist brochures for an automobile association in Chicago, I think . . .

WELLES: Friends?

JANET: She didn't seem to have friends. I mean, no one that visited her often or called her . . .

WELLES: No phone calls?

JANET: No one called that I know of.

WELLES: Not even about work?

JANET: No. Not at all, except there was one time I heard her make a call . . .

WELLES: Do you remember who it was to?

JANET: It was so unusual I was curious. I couldn't help hearing — she was talking to someone named Alvy. They made a date to meet at a downtown cafe. I don't remember which one or maybe I never knew . . .

WELLES: And what can you tell me about her habits?

JANET: I beg your pardon . . . ?

WELLES: She was full of coke when we found her.

JANET: I heard that! And I'm totally surprised! Ruth never took drugs!

WELLES: How do you know?

JANET: Living together . . . how could she hide it — especially in such a small apartment!

WELLES: Maybe she took them when you were away.

JANET: I don't think so, I hardly ever go out and neither did she. She usually worked at home.

WELLES: *(Looking into her eyes.)* How friendly were the two of you?

JANET: I don't understand the question.

WELLES: You were together all the time, you must have confided in each other.

JANET: No. Ruth was very reserved.

WELLES: In all that time you never exchanged even one secret?

(Janet shakes her head. Welles stares at her fixedly. Janet doesn't meet his gaze and is uncomfortable.)

WELLES: How close were you, really?

JANET: We weren't that close. It was only a casual friendship.

WELLES: But you would have liked to have been closer to her, isn't that right?

JANET: *(Upset.)* What are you trying to get at, Commissioner?

WELLES: Why were you at the Motel?

JANET: What?? I . . . I went for Ruth . . . She was supposed to come back that night. I got worried when she didn't and in the morning when I heard the news, her description . . . *(She breaks down.)* . . . I had a horrible premonition, so instead of going to the University, I went to the motel . . .

WELLES: Was that the first time she was out all night?

JANET: No. She'd done it before, Twice. But she always told me beforehand.

WELLES: Do you have premonitions often?

JANET: *(Tense.)* Why?

WELLES: Do you know how far it is from your apartment to the motel?

JANET: Not exactly. It's . . . a little far.

WELLES: It's fifteen miles. Do you want me to believe that you drove fifteen miles and skipped your classes because of a premonition?

JANET: She was my roommate.

WELLES: Bullshit! The description of Ruth on television was very vague. You couldn't really make her out in the photos. No. I think you went there because you knew it was her. Because somehow you knew that your friend was in danger or maybe because you're implicated in her murder!

JANET: No!

WELLES: Talk to me or I'll have to lock you up!

JANET: OKAY . . . all right . . . I suppose you could say that . . . last night when she went out, she seemed very worried . . . she asked me to do her a big favor. She gave me a small key and told me that in case something happened to her, I should go get some letters out of a locker at the Greyhound terminal in St. Louis and mail them. She also asked me to swear that for nothing in this world would I mention this to anyone . . . I became very alarmed, and when she didn't return last night . . . *(She sobs.)* I shouldn't have let her go out last night. I should never have let her!

WELLES: Where's the key? Do you have it with you?

JANET: I hid it at the apartment. I'll bring it to you this afternoon.

(Janet leaves the office. On the television a sentence appears. "Scandal in the White House.")

JACK: Yesterday's edition of the Lebanese newspaper Al-Shiraa stated that the United States has been selling arms secretly to Iran and that part of the funds from those sales has been sent to help the Contras. President Reagan and his associates deny any knowledge of such a situation.

(Commissioner Welles' office. The door opens and O'Hara enters with Carlos Gonzalez who is furious.)

WELLES: Please, have a seat. I'm Commissioner Welles. I'd like to ask you a couple questions . . .

(Carlos pulls himself away from O'Hara and comes towards Welles.)

CARLOS: No. You're the one who's going to give me an explanation, right now! Why have you had me arrested?

WELLES: Detained.

CARLOS: Fuck you. Arrested, kept incommunicado and without even knowing what crime I've been accused of!

WELLES: Your detention is related to the murder of Ruth Gordon.

CARLOS: *(The news surprises him.)* She's been killed?

WELLES: You didn't know? Well, that's why you're here. Your name was in the victim's date book.

CARLOS: And since when is it a crime to be in someone's appointment book?

WELLES: The book was new. There were only three names in it. Yours was one of them.

CARLOS: Lucky for you. What if she'd been found clutching a telephone book?

WELLES: This is no joking matter.

CARLOS: Well don't be stupid! Look at what you're doing. This is illegal.

WELLES: We're following the legal process fixed by the law in criminal cases concerning drugs.

CARLOS: I know the law and I also know my rights. If you're accusing me of something, do it right now. Otherwise I demand my immediate release for lack of cause!

WELLES: I'm sorry, but you'll have to wait.

CARLOS: I hope you're aware that holding me incommunicado without legal cause is a flagrant violation of international law. This is going to create a diplomatic conflict at a very high level.

O'HARA: With Mexico? Oh, I'm shaking in my boots.

WELLES: Jesus, O'Hara! *(To Carlos.)* We'll have to run that risk. Things connected with drugs are a very delicate matter here in the States . . . be patient. We'll treat you like a high government official who's been invited to collaborate with us.

CARLOS: Invited my ass! I still don't understand how you could be so stupid as to bring me here without even advising the embassy . . . *(He sees the telephone and picks it up.)* . . . but you could still do it . . .
(Welles disconnects the phone.)

CARLOS: I demand you let me speak with my embassy, right now!

WELLES: I'm sorry, but I can't do that for now.

CARLOS: Then it's over. I'm leaving and you can only stop me by using violence. Let this matter be handled at the highest level of our government.
(He starts to leave and O'Hara stops him.)

CARLOS: You touch me and we'll see how long you last in your job — you sack of lard!
(He pushes O'Hara aside and starts to leave when Welles grabs him by the collar and turns him around. Welles knees him in the stomach and gives him a karate blow to the neck. Carlos falls heavily to the floor.)

WELLES: Take him back to his cell until he's in a better mood. Bring me Nick Gomez. I want to interrogate him.

JACK: Now, international news: A Southern Air plane, transporting arms to the Contras, crashed as it was taking off from the San Antonio airport today; one day earlier another plane, a C-123K containing arms and a supply of a thousand ammunitions, was shot down in the southern tip of Nicaragua. Eugene Hasenfus, the only survivor, was captured by the Sandinastas, who are now protesting the participation of the White House, through the CIA, in terrorist activities and supplying arms to the rebels.

ON SCREEN: *Hasenfrus claims to have received direct instructions from Vice President Bush.*

(We see Nicaraguan President Daniel Ortega on television.)

ORTEGA: Despite the prohibition by Congress, the White House continues to send more arms than ever to the Contras!

JACK: The White House denies all charges

ON SCREEN: *Countries supplying arms, money or training to the Contras during this prohibition were China, Israel, England, Ireland, Brunei, Saudi Arabia, all the Central American countries except Panama under the government of Noriega.*

(Change to a photograph of the murder victim Ruth Gordon.)

JACK: No suspects have been found in the murder at the Motel Paisano Drive. Four individuals have been taken into custody in connection with the crime as the investigation continues.

(At the jail, a white spotlight illuminates Nick's face.)

NICK: I met her about a month ago. It was a Sunday afternoon . . .

(Lights up on Nick's Cafe. Ruth enters.)

NICK: She arrived alone, dressed all in white, like a dream. The whole place fell quiet as she passed.

(Ruth sits down at a table. Nick hurries over with the menu.)

NICK: Good evening, miss. What can I do for you?

(Ruth takes the menu and look it over.)

RUTH: Son buenos aqui los nachos?

NICK: Muy buenos, senorita *(To Welles.)* — She really spoke Spanish well, you know *(To Ruth.)* — Son la especialidad de la casa!

RUTH: Bueno. Quiero "Nachos" y una cerveza mexicana — la que sea.

(Nick writes down the order and goes towards the kitchen.)

NICK: Such a beautiful elegant woman couldn't pass unnoticed. Plus, before I could warn her, she went into the men's john. She didn't seem to notice the charro's sombrero on the door.

(Nick sees her enter and doesn't know what to do.)

NICK: What I did was stand by the door so no one else would go in. I stood there quite a while until, a little worried, I knocked on the door, softly, you know, just to see if she was all right.

(The door opens and Ruth appears smiling. She sees Nick waiting there.)

RUTH: It looks like I made a mistake. And you were watching out for me. How sweet.

(She returns to her table. Nick brings her the nachos. Ruth flirts with him. The man becomes nervous.)

RUTH: Thanks. Won't you sit down? I hate eating alone.

(Nick starts to sit down but then changes his mind.)

NICK: No. Well yes — I was going to sit down with her, but when I thought it over, I realized my wife could come in and see us from the kitchen . . . so I thought better of it, better not. *(To Ruth.)* You know, I have to keep an eye on the kitchen . . . but here I am.

(He stands next to her, Ruth looks at him smiling while she eats. The man is fascinated by the young woman.)

RUTH: Mmmm . . . The nachos are delicious.

NICK: You really like them?

RUTH: They're the best!

NICK: Well yes — my old la . . . my old cook does a good job. I taught her how to make them myself.

RUTH: I wish you would show me too!

NICK: Well . . . sure . . . whenever you want!

(The young woman eats. Nick decides to continue the chat.)

NICK: On vacation?

RUTH: No. Working. I've been asked to write a pamphlet for tourists on this city . . . and the first thing I'm going to recommend in it are your nachos.

NICK: Great . . . great . . .*(To Welles.)* The wench had a good sense of humor, I'll give her that . . . *(To Ruth.)* I hope you keep visiting us.

RUTH: The nachos are great, but . . . I can't recommend your bathrooms.

(She sees the embarrassed look on the man's face and adds, smiling.)

Don't feel bad, I know how difficult it is to keep them clean — but look what I found on the floor!

(She shows him the butt of a marijuana cigarette.)

NICK: *(Mortified.)* A joint of grass. It's hard to prevent that. All kinds of people come here. I don't let anyone smoke any of that garbage here in the restaurant, but in the bathroom . . .

RUTH: Don't worry. There's nothing wrong with marijuana — actually its good for calming your nerves and for rheumatism . . . and for making love.

NICK: And she looked deep into my eyes while my pulse was going a hundred miles a minute. I think she noticed that I was blown away, because she asked me —

RUTH: Is something wrong?

NICK: No . . . no . . . I was just thinking about . . . the marijuana.

RUTH: Is it easy to find around here?

NICK: I don't know. Since I don't smoke . . .

RUTH: But surely you know people who do, in the bathroom . . . and the people who sell it, no?

NICK: Well I have some idea . . . but I'm not sure . . .

RUTH: If you figure out how I might get some, a little, I'd be very grateful . . .
(She puts her hand over Nick's trembling hand and adds:)

RUTH: Of course, all this is just between me and you.

NICK: *(To the commissioner.)* Sure I knew some pushers — even not wanting to — you hear about a lot of things at the cafe. I put her in contact with the two best known ones . . . but what's this all about? Did something happen to her?

WELLES: Yeah. They hung her.

NICK: Ay dios, no . . . no please. No, no . . .
(The telephone rings. The commissioner answers it.)

WELLES: Commissioner Welles speaking. Yes. Who's this? . . . oh yeah, Bill, what is it? What? Are you sure? Who was it? Bullshit Where are you now? *(He writes.)* Peyote Street between Main and Second. Don't you move until I get there. Damnit . . . Damnit!
(He rings a buzzer and Sergeant O'Hara enters.)

WELLES: Janet Falco was run over by a drunk and she's dead. Take this guy away and come with me. I'll wait for you downstairs.
(He takes his raincoat and exits.)

JACK: The Iran Contra Affair is getting complicated; President Reagan is complaining about being betrayed by the National Security Council; Poindexter is complaining about being betrayed by Secretary of State Shultz, who for his part is blaming the director of the CIA for having pulled the wool over his eyes. The Secretary of American Affairs, Elliot Abrahms, is very remorseful about having fooled Congress; McFarlane, for having fooled the American public; and finally sixty-three percent of the population doesn't believe the president was really trying to fool anyone in the Iran

Contra Affair — since everyone knew from the beginning that President Reagan was hiding the truth . . .

(In an alley, Commissioner Welles slaps around a drunk.)

WELLES: Tell me. Why did you kill her?

DRUNK: It was an accident. I don't know how it happened. I lost control of the car. I don't know why. I only had two beers . . . I ain't drunk!

WELLES: Your plates are from Kansas. What're you doing in Missouri?

DRUNK: I came to Saint Louis, a big jazz blowout . . . I'm a musician, I was going home.

WELLES: Yeah well the highway from St. Louis to Kansas is Route 70. So what're you doing on Route 54?

DRUNK: I don't know . . . I don't know . . .

WELLES: Why did you go to Mexico?

DRUNK: I dunno . . .

WELLES: Where were you going when you ran over her?

DRUNK: Look, I dunno . . . I don't know nothing *(He cries.)* I'm innocent!

JACK: And now our international news . . .

(Photograph of Colombia with the phrase: More than 15,000 assassinations so far this year . . .)

JACK: Today in Columbia the leader of the Leftist Party was assassinated and the most important sculptor in the country was kidnapped. Sixteen people were gunned down last night by drug dealers in downtown Bogota. This brings the total killed to more than 1200 during the month of October. In what is being touted as the most violent escalation of crime in this country since 1954, the greater part of the Colombian artists and intellectuals have received death threats as have most judges and personnel of the Justice Department.

(Photos illustrate his narrative.)

JACK: The violence seems to be principally the work of the drug mafias who last year murdered one of the ministers of justice, more than twenty judges and a half a dozen journalists who dared to challenge their power . . .

(A white light illuminates the face of Alvaro Gallegos.)

AL: The name in that women's date book wasn't mine; it was my son's. He has the same name. But yes I knew her, yes she was in our house several times . . . when Alvy brought her over the first time, we thought she was one of his teachers from College. We treated her extremely well. Afterwards, we realized that her interest in Alvy had nothing to do with his studies. That's when I decided to have a talk with him. Give him some advice. . . .

(Lights up on an area of the Gallegos house.)

AL: No and that's it! Do not bring that woman back to this house!

ALVY: What're you getting so upset about, Papa? There's no reason to make such a big fuss.

AL: That woman is a lot older than you! *(To Welles.)* Something told me that my son would be in danger if he stayed around her. Plus she was a total stranger.

ALVY: Who cares if she's older. We're only friends.

AL: Friends? Sure. I know what that woman wants from you!

ALVY: Papa, be real. I'm twenty-two years old, for godsake. You can't keep treating me like I'm a child.

AL: Well then, don't act like a child.

ALVY: At least respect my right to choose my own friends!

AL: You earn your rights — by being responsible and exercising good judgement. Whims are only that . . . whims, fantasy . . . which I don't have to accept or tolerate!

ALVY: You're still in Mexico in the fifties, Papa — that's your problem. You just want to control all of us!

AL: How dare you speak to me that way!

ALVY: You insist on rules that make no sense nowadays, in this country. You've got to adapt, Papa or you're going to fuck us all up.

AL: I forbid you to use that language with me!

ALVY: Look what you've done with my sister, with your authoritarianism. She's like a mental retard, who can't do anything on her own.

AL: That's enough!

(He tries to hit Alvy but his son stops him.)

ALVY: No, Papa. No more hitting. I always avoided confronting you, I don't know why. It was easier, or I didn't want to cause a scene, maybe because I love you and tried to believe that everything you did was because you thought it was best, but you've gone too far, Papa. Maybe cause you're unhappy. You're getting worse and I'm not going to let you take out your frustrations on us — we've got enough of our own to deal with. I love Ruth, Papa, a lot. You're right about that part . . .

AL: You see? I knew it!

ALVY: But it's my problem. She doesn't even know . . . and I don't think she'd be interested anyway . . .

(The dialogue is interrupted by footsteps in the hall that distract them. Ruth appears.)

RUTH: Good afternoon.

AL: Miss Gordon. It's good you're here, we were just talking about you.

ALVY: Papa!

RUTH: About me? You're making me feel very important from the sound of your argument. I could hear it from the street.

AL: Look, I don't know if you already have children.

RUTH: No, and I'm starting to worry about that.

AL: *(Without hearing her.)* Well someday you'll have them, and then you'll understand how difficult it is to raise them decently. Perhaps then you'll understand what I'm about to say.

RUTH: You're having trouble with your son? *(Jokes with Alvy.)* . . . You nasty boy! *(To the father.)* Well fortunately your job with him is done. He's reached adulthood and it seems like you raised him very well; that you've been a very good father. Now it's his turn to pass on what you've taught him.

AL: You're a very intelligent woman, very shrewd. Now I see you've wrapped my son around your little finger.

ALVY: Oh shit!

RUTH: Truthfully, I would have preferred to unwrap him.

AL: *(Loses it.)* Justamente! That's precisely what I was talking about. I'm trying to keep my son, who's a good decent kid, from the clutches of sluts like you!

ALVY: No! Papa! How could you say that?!

RUTH: Your father's having a hard time right now, but he's a good responsible man who loves you a lot . . . I should go — walk me to the door? *(To Al.)* Thank you for your hospitality and kindness, good evening.

(She exits. Alvy doesn't know what to do. He's ashamed and embarrassed.)

ALVY: Oh Papa. Poor Papa. *(He follows her.)*

AL: That was the last time I knew anything about her until today!

WELLES: And your son? What can you tell me about him?

AL: My son?

WELLES: Where is he?

AL: I don't know. At home, I suppose, if he's already finished with his classes today . . .

WELLES: Are you saying that after your little talk with him, he gave up Ruth Gordon and became an exemplary son?

AL: Why the irony, sir?

WELLES: What the hell's the matter with you?

AL: *(Upset.)* Why?

WELLES: You've been sitting here deliberately lying to me all this time . . . what do you hope to gain? Do you want me to charge you with perjury?

AL: Well . . . could you explain what you mean?

WELLES: First you lied to me about his using drugs. You actually swore that no one in your family uses drugs.

AL: I still say that!

(The commissioner takes out a report from his desk drawer.)

WELLES: Isn't your son Alvaro Gallegos Salazar? *(Al sits down.)* Well, here I have a report from Memorial Hospital where he was admitted three times for drug addiction.

AL: Let me correct you, sir. He was admitted for migraines. My son suffers very painful attacks. Since my wife works at that hospital, she took him there so she could attend him personally.

(The commissioner squints at him curiously.)

WELLES: So he had migraines . . . Tell me, did you ever take him to the hospital?

AL: I can't. I've got very restrictive work hours.

(Welles vacillates. He's disconcerted by Alvaro's sincerity and vehemence.)

WELLES: Well look, I don't know your family situation, or how they've managed to keep everything from you, if you truly are in the dark. What I can tell you for sure is that your son was taking drugs before, he's taking them now, and I have some cause to think he might be connected to a local drug dealer.

AL: It can't be.

WELLES: On the other hand, drugs are expensive, and I don't think you could have or would have given him enough money to keep him in drugs.

AL: *(Very pale.)* Can I see the hospital report?

(Welles gives it to him.)

WELLES: The rest of your lies . . . well . . . your son hasn't been home for a few days and you know it — but perhaps you wanted to keep that secret because you too had some suspicions about it; that your son was with Ruth in the motel, that they took drugs, they fought and he killed her!

AL: *(Softly. Almost calmly.)* No, Alvy would never do anything like that.

WELLES: Well, that's our version, at least for now. We still haven't found your son, Ruth's SUV, and other details that might confirm it. It's a question of time . . . and not very much time.

(The TV turns on. We see Jack Colby and the words: Drug production increases worldwide.)

JACK COLBY: The State Department said today that despite the economic and technical aid it has given to many countries to fight drugs, the production of cocaine is up 40 percent from the last four years; marijuana is up

20 percent and heroine 50 percent. Faced with this situation, President Reagan sent an amendment to the Senate that would allow him to stop economic aid to all countries that, in his judgment, encouraged drug production or were not making a major effort to attack the problem.

REAGAN: Why should we help nations which are the source of poisoning and corrupting our youth? I'm only waiting for Senate approval to suspend credit to Peru, Colombia, Bolivia, Brazil and Argentina . . .

JACK: The reaction of the countries affected by this decision was immediate!

(On screen: In the United Nations, Latin American Diplomats Protest.)

COLUMBIA: We can never solve the drug problem in our countries while the United States maintains the largest open market for drugs in the world!

JACK: A communique from the Anti-Drug Intelligence Committee informed us that the consumption of drugs in the U.S. continues to climb; marijuana by 50 percent a year, heroine by 2 percent, and cocaine, ever more popular in our country, by 12 percent.

(On Screen: 56 percent of the crimes in New York City involve drugs.)

MEXICO: President Reagan's threat to cancel loans to Mexico for supposed lack of cooperation, forces us to make the following statement: We are focusing fifty percent of our attorney general's annual budget to combat drug trafficking. What's more, you can count in the hundreds the number of our agents who've been killed in this war on drugs. I ask what spectacular results can the United States show in their actions against the drug mafias that operate within their frontiers?

JACK: President Reagan and members of his cabinet are sending urine samples to be tested to prove that none of them have tried drugs. And as an example of national civic feeling, they have also initiated educational programs throughout the country.

(A black man mimes offering a syringe to a little girl in front of a poster with the famous phrase, "Just Say No.")

ARGENTINA: You think that's going to solve the drug problem? What idiots!

BRAZIL: If you fought drugs as hard as you fight communism — you'd have the drug problem taken care of by now.

PERU: You have to begin by helping us with an external debt that makes it impossible for us to generate jobs for the more than 300,000 peasants employed in the production of cocaine — and so we can pay an honest and more efficient police force.

DEA: If you'd just let us help you — you wouldn't need more police.

AMNESTY INTERNATIONAL: Under the guise of creating these forces to combat drugs, Guatemala, Argentina and Brazil created "Death Squads."

CIA: I suggest that the Latin American governments supported by our agents toughen their stance against the guerrillas, since they're the ones who consume the most drugs. By fighting the guerrillas, you'll also be fighting drugs.

NICARAGUA: Is that true for us as well?

CIA: Not in your case. Your government favors Soviet leadership.

NICARAGUA: That's a lie! There's not one country in Latin America that prefers Soviet leadership. You're the ones who force us in this direction. And under the pretense of fighting communism, prolong our wars and sell more weapons.

(On Screen: The White House announces a ninety percent cutback in Nicaragua's sugar quota.)

JACK: The Senate has approved President Reagan's initiative on the drug problem in Latin America. And Mrs. Hawkins, the senator from Florida, is the first to apply it.

HAWKINS: We are informing President Siles Zuago of Bolivia that as a result of his lukewarm collaboration in our fight against drugs, the fifty-seven million dollar loan they requested for development programs is being denied.

(The office of Roberto Suarez, Colombian drug dealer.)

ROBERTO: Tell Siles, I'll loan him two thousand million dollars for his development programs. At a lower interest and whenever he wants them.

(In his cell. Carlos has finished writing out a document.)

CARLOS: There it is! If everyone signs this, it'll be a diplomatic bomb!

(He passes the document to Alvaro who doesn't know what to do with it.)

AL: And this?

CARLOS: Read it and sign it. *(To the others.)* I'm going to send this to *The New York Times*, *The Wall Street Journal* and to Notimex in Mexico. We're going to cause a huge fucking scandal!

AL: *(Reading.)* But . . . I can't sign this.

CARLOS: Why not?

AL: I don't want to have any problems when I get out of here.

CARLOS: You don't have to get out of here to have problems. You've got them right now.

AL: Yeah — but this is temporary. Everything will be cleared up and they'll let us go.

CARLOS: What about what they've done to us already?

AL: You're a bigwig in the government. You'll go back to Mexico and in a couple of weeks — everything will be forgotten. But for us . . . well, we'll be staying here, this is where our families, our houses are . . . do you understand?

CARLOS: So?

NICK: What the man's trying to tell you is that we have things to protect.

CARLOS: Right! And the way to protect your property and your families is to defend your rights! I mean . . . why the hell do they have us here? Why only us? Do you think for a moment that if that lady's famous appointment book had had gringo names in it, that they would have put the gringos in jail? No! They're racist. That's why we're here. It's the way they've always done things and they'll keep on doing them that way if we let them!

AL: You're probably right and please forgive me for not signing that letter. I have personal reasons for not doing it.

CARLOS: What about you?

NICK: I can't. I got a business that cost me a lot to get going. If I sign that — I'll have problems. I know it. Those white guys are real shrewd. They'll find a way to get back at me. I'd rather live in peace.

CARLOS: And you think that by renouncing your rights, they'll let you live in peace? You must be kidding — you're Mexican and worse — a wetback! They'll keep screwing you.

NICK: I'M NOT A MEXICAN. I'M AN AMERICAN CITIZEN.

CARLOS: No shit. Have you looked in the mirror lately? You look like Tlaloc.

NICK: But my children were born here!

CARLOS: The Sioux Indians were born here too and look what happened to them! Well if you're chickening out — I'm going to send it anyways.
(Tiro approaches trembling with rage.)

TIRO: I ain't backing out. Why are you calling all of us chickens. I'll sign it!
(Carlos is surprised, smiles and passes him the document. Tiro scribbles his mark. Nick comes up.)

NICK: Well . . . I'll sign it too — maybe we'll see each other on the other side, brother.
(After the three sign, they turn and look at Al, who vacillates but finally turns away from them. O'Hara enters.)

O'HARA: Alvarro . . . Galigous?

AL: Yes sir.

O'HARA: Follow me.

AL: Whatever you say, sir.
(They exit and go to the commissioner's office. We see Oliver North on the screen.)

NORTH: My concern was always with those people who were fighting the most extraordinary fight for liberty on our continent. I'm convinced, just like the president, that the end of the Contras will mean the end of Central America, then Mexico and then the United States.

JACK: After being accused of diverting funds from arm sales to Iran to help the Contras, Lieutenant Colonel North posed some hard questions to the congressmen in his defense before Congress.

NORTH: What else could we do, faced with a fickle, vacillating Congress that was insensitive to the enormous dangers the Sandinistas pose to our security?

JACK: He also contested the accusations that he misused funds. When they accused him of having lied to Congress and the public, and of having destroyed valuable documents and official memoranda that would have clarified the trial, North replied . . .

NORTH: I did it so there would be no leaks from Congress which might endanger the life and patrimony of the people who have collaborated with us in this risky business of saving the hostages in Teheran and saving Nicaragua and the rest of the Americas from international communism . . .

JACK: Finally he exonerated President Reagan.

NORTH: He never ordered me to divert those funds or to give assistance to these defenders of liberty; but I'm sure that I acted in accordance with his desires and always with the help and guidance of God . . .

JACK: The words of this new American leader have gained wide support. And now, before continuing with our programming, an announcement. We are now offering Oliver North T-shirts for sale to our television audience.
(He tries one on as Alvaro enters Welles' office.)

AL: So, how can I help you, sir?

WELLES: Come in. Come in. Please have a seat . . . I'd like you to look at something.

AL: Of course, sir.

WELLES: Would you like a drink?

AL: Well, thank you, but I don't drink.
(The commissioner pours him a drink.)

WELLES: Better drink this. You're going to need it.
(Alvaro doesn't know quite what to do with the drink. Welles turns up the volume on the TV where we see Jack trying on his T-shirt.)

AL: I don't understand what you mean, sir.
(Welles signals him to wait a moment. The TV changes. Now we see a photo of the motel with the words: Light in the Ruth Gordon Case.)

JACK: Ruth Gordon's SUV has finally been found in the outskirts of Waco — some eight miles from here.

(While the announcer continues narrating the news, the camera pulls in closer and closer to the vehicle until we can see the interior.)

JACK: The body of a young man was found with one bullet in his chest and a .38 at his side. The bullets from the gun were the same as the one that killed him.

(The camera focuses on the dead youth's face and we hear a muffled scream. Alvaro falls to the floor, sobbing convulsively. Welles hurries over to help him. He gives him a little whiskey. The reporter on TV continues.)

JACK: It has been deemed an apparent suicide. This was the young man who was with Ruth Gordon the night of the crime

(On Screen: Jack interviews Bill.)

BILL: Right. This is considered a suicide. He was drugged. We found traces of coke in his nose and under his nails. And we found the motel key in his pocket . . .

JACK: An older couple called in the police.

OLD MAN: The car was parked there for a couple days. So finally we decided to take a closer look . . .

(Welles turns off the TV. Alvaro gets himself somewhat under control.)

AL: Son . . . my son! . . .

WELLES: *(To O'Hara.)* Confirmed. It's Alvy Galigous.

AL: Why have you been so cruel to me?

WELLES: We had to be sure it was him.

AL: God — why do you punish me like this? Why don't you kill me instead?

(He cries uncontrollably. The commissioner gives him sips of whiskey.)

AL: I built my whole life around him. We came here for him, to protect him. To give him a better life. In Mexico I was a medical researcher at the University. Here I'm only some lowly pharmaceutical salesman . . . and now this!

WELLES: I think this ends our investigation.

(He looks to O'Hara for agreement. O'Hara nods.)

WELLES: The Intelligence agents should be here any minute. As soon as they give us the word, you'll be free to go. You'll be free to attend your son's burial. *(To O'Hara.)* Take him away so he can start getting his things together.

(Alvaro gets up painfully and goes to the door. He stops as if his mind registered something surprising, unusual, brutal. He begins shaking again.)

WELLES: Are you all right?

(With great difficulty, Al turns around.)

AL: Excuse me, Commissioner . . . would it be too much to ask . . . I'd like to see my son again . . . please!

WELLES: Of course . . . *(Keeping his eyes on Al, he calls through the intercom.)* Please play that videotape again. The part that shows the interior of the SUV . . . *(To Alvaro.)* . . . Did you see something?

AL: No . . . it's only . . . it was so . . . I'd just like to see him one last time, that's all . . . there he is!

WELLES: Hold it there! . . . Is that what you wanted to see?

(On seeing the photo, Al can't control the tics that accumulate on his face. He begins to moan low, like a wounded animal. He goes towards the exit. Welles stops him.)

WELLES: Wait a minute . . . What did you see?

(O'Hara intercepts him and Alvaro pushes him away furiously.)

AL: Murderer! . . . *(He turns to Welles.)* Murderers!

(He tries to leave but Welles goes to the door and confronts him.)

WELLES: What did you see?

AL: Now I understand everything!

WELLES: What do you understand?

AL: That you guys killed my son!

O'HARA: Us?

AL: *(Beside himself.)* Yes — so you could blame him and he couldn't defend himself. I don't know who you're trying to protect . . . but you're wrong about my son! My son was left-handed . . . he couldn't have killed himself in the way you're trying to make it appear!

(The police look at each other.)

AL: But things won't stay this way, you'll see, I'm going to send letters to the papers . . . I'll demand another investigation. You'll be sorry for what you've done! You'll be sorry! *(He's hysterical.)*

(Welles slaps him and Alvaro throws himself on the sofa sobbing like a child. Welles makes a sign to O'Hara to take him away. O'Hara leaves with Alvaro, who is destroyed. Welles goes up to the photo and scrutinizes it awhile. He gets an idea. He talks through the intercom.)

WELLES: Bill, get my car. We're going to Ruth Gordon's apartment!

(He grabs his raincoat and leaves the office.)

END OF ACT ONE

ACT TWO

The president before Congress.

REAGAN: I've been brought up to date on the Contras and yes, those freedom fighters were receiving economic aid from us, as well as third party countries and private companies who are sympathetic to their just cause. I am guilty of that, although I didn't know that funds from arms sales to Iran were being sent to those patriots. I take responsibility for my associates, who in good faith and in an effort to protect me, did keep me in the dark about their plans. This is unfortunate because no president should be protected from the truth . . .

(In Ruth's apartment, the commissioner looks for the key Janet had mentioned before her death. Bill watches him curiously.)

BILL: Could you tell me what you're looking for, Commissioner?

WELLES: Nothing in particular. I just wanted to look the place over. Doesn't it seem strange to you that everything is so neat, everything in it's place? Look, even the plants seem to have been watered recently . . . well, not all of them.

(All of a sudden he notices something. He looks over one of the plants more carefully. He looks up and sees Bill watching him vacantly.)

WELLES: Go see if there's hot water in the bathroom

(Puzzled, Bill accepts the order and goes. Welles takes advantage of the moment to remove a small bag from the bottom of the plant — a plastic bag which was keeping the water from draining out. He finds the key to the locker inside. Bill comes back and Welles hides the key.)

BILL: Yeah, everything's working fine. I mean . . .

WELLES: I thought so. Well, let's get our of here — there's nothing here. Look — you can go eat, I've got some errands to do. I'll see you later at the office.

(On television, Reagan continues his speech:)

REAGAN: Poindexter, North and Casey himself believed they were doing what I would have wanted them to do — prevent the Russians from setting up a beachhead in our own backyard.

(Bus terminal, a bank of storage lockers. Welles arrives, opens a locker and takes out a canvas bag in which he finds clothes, a wig that he examines very carefully. He also finds documents, identification and credentials which surprise him.)

(He notices a package of envelopes and hides them in his suit coat pocket. He

puts back everything the way it was. He wipes off his fingerprints with a hand-kerchief; locks the locker, and throws the key down a drain. He walks hur-riedly away.)

REAGAN: However, they're good people, whose only error was overstepping the law in order to follow what they considered their duty; I believe they shouldn't be brought to trial, because they did act in the best interest of our country . . .

(Welles arrives at his office, takes out the packet of envelopes and with great excitement begins to read them. In a ghostly light, the dead woman narrates what he is reading.)

HELEN: If you're reading this letter, it means that I'm dead, murdered and that I didn't even know by whom . . .

(Still reading, Welles takes off his coat and throws it on an old coatrack with-out even looking. He goes to sit down.)

HELEN: My name is Helen Esparza. I'm a chicana, daughter and granddaughter of chicanos. I've also used the names Ruth Gordon, Diana Rand, Rosa de Guadalajara and others that I don't remember right now. Reason? My work. I'm an agent with the DEA in Chicago, at least I was until this last month . . . the same as my father Joe Esparza who was murdered by the drug mafia a couple years ago.

(Welles takes out a bottle of whiskey and pours himself a generous portion.)

HELEN: I am writing this letter to get the support of your prestigious *New York Times* so this investigation, which I began two years ago and was on the verge of tying up, can be continued. We must stop the unloading of the largest shipment of drugs ever sent to our country. Tons of coke and hero-ine will be deposited in the very heart of Missouri and from there dis-tributed from coast to coast, poisoning young people throughout the United States.

(It's begun to get dark. Welles turns on the light.)

HELEN: I'll try to give you a chronology of events so you can take up my in-vestigation where I left off and can verify the truth of my sources. It all began in Columbia, at the first signs of spring. I had been sent there on my own personal initiative because of a sudden spectacular increase in drug production

(On screen we find the following information on Columbia: From 1981–1986 the cocaine production grew from four to fifteen tons and the growing area from 4,000 to 20,000 hectares . . .)

HELEN: I met an exceptional man in Columbia. The minister of the Supreme Court. I presented myself to him as Diana Rand, a journalist . . .

(As she is speaking she puts on a red wig, glasses and low-heeled shoes. She enters the Supreme Court justice's office and sits in front of his desk. She takes notes.)

DIANA: You were saying before that the drug trafficking problem can't be resolved as long as the United States offers such an open market.

MINISTER: Yes. I believe that. The drug business functions in the classic capitalist mode — responds to the principle of supply and demand.

DIANA: What about each country's official controls?

MINISTER: Truthfully? They're useless when it comes to drugs. Drugs have the capacity to generate such huge profits that they can quite easily pay the cost of operating illegally and can survive any repression — national or international.

DIANA: Are you telling me, as a Supreme Court justice, that your government cannot control the drug trade?

MINISTER: The economic power of the Medellin Cartel greatly exceeds that of any Colombian ministry. Income from drug exportation comes to thousands of millions of dollars. This allows the drug lords to influence our system to such a degree that our State and our economy have begun to depend on this new power — the narcosystem . . .

HELEN: Do you think that a situation similar to Columbia is actually arising in the United States?

MINISTER: I think it has already begun. If economic growth in Columbia depends on the crumbs of profit from the wholesale production and distribution of drugs, imagine the financial power of those who control the retail circulation and consumption of drugs — in the very heart of the largest drug market in the world.

(On Screen: The approximate annual value of drugs in the United States is between 100 to 500 thousand million dollars a year. The wholesalers that distribute it keep about eighty percent. The exporters and intermediaries get about 18.5 percent and the growers keep 1.5 percent. Another odd fact — a drug addict spends about twenty-five million pesos a year (1987) in buying drugs.)

DIANA: Well, is there something you in Columbia can do?

MINISTER: We're doing what we can. However, to close off this non sancta source of foreign currency when we have an external debt of 15 thousand million dollars, isn't an easy job . . . we're pressured on all sides — the social and political costs are unpredictable, unimaginable . . . our work would be made simpler if we could count on the US.

DIANA: Don't you count on them already?

MINISTER: Not in a significant way, no.

DIANA: According to some statistical information I have available, the U.S. government has invested 200 million dollars a year in other countries — yours included — to fight drug trafficking.

(On Screen: 12.7 million dollars to Columbia in 1986.)

MINISTER: Your government is more interested in fighting the siren song of communism than in fighting drug trafficking.

(W. Casey, director of the CIA, makes a comment.)

CASEY: The drug mafia doesn't represent a real problem for our country. Right now — communism does. Communism is infiltrating the heart of our nation. The drug lords might even prove to be formidable allies in fighting this menace.

(All of a sudden he has a stroke and dies. Two women enter dressed in black and stand by his side with a large sign that says Don't send flowers to my funeral, send money to support the Contras in Nicaragua.)

MINISTER: Furthermore, the United States wouldn't have to invest so much in other countries if they would only control their own mafias and take better care of drug addiction. If their internal consumption of drugs decreases, so would worldwide production of drugs.

DIANA: You think they haven't done that?

MINISTER: Let's say, they haven't done it enough.

DIANA: What makes you believe that?

MINISTER: It's a question of economics — as it is with the arms industry. The drug business allows Americans to maintain a high standard of living. Therefore people who are reasonably happy with their economic situation, misinformed and with ever-diminishing spiritual concerns, don't protest . . .

HOUSEWIFE: Look, as long as I've got money in my pocket — let the politicians take care of our country's problems.

MINISTER: The drug trade is also a source of financial contributions for political campaigns . . .

(On Screen: Reagan and Bush received financial support from known drug mafias in their campaigns and forty percent of the Colombian parliament has received some financial aid from the Cartel in their campaigns . . .)

MINISTER: And influences lobbyists on policies to other countries.

R SINGER: In the next few years, instead of sending in the Marines, Washington will send anti-drug agents to defend their private interests.

MINISTER: Otherwise how do you account for their lack of success? They surely have the means and the information to do it.

DIANA: How do you know they have the right information?

MINISTER: I know in the case of Columbia — I gave it to them personally.

(The young woman is surprised and the minister smiles.)

I can recite by heart the names of the major drug lords in Columbia, their locations, their income, their agents . . . even their contacts in the U.S. . . .

(He takes a check out of his desk and waves it in front of the young woman.)

MINISTER: This check was sent to me by the Medellin Cartel to finance my campaign for congressman, and of course, so I would shut up about what I know . . .

DIANA: Could I get a hold of this information?

MINISTER: Yes, with an official request. In your case, it would be through your newspaper.

DIANA: In my case, it would be a personal request . . .

MINISTER: *(Surprised.)* And why would you want it?

DIANA: To infiltrate the heart of the drug mafia and write a firsthand account. To show my country the real face of drug trafficking in Columbia; it's mechanisms of operation and corruption; it's relationship with the United States . . . very little is known there about all this . . . I mean, statistics are published, but not in a meaningful context. I want to create a burning awareness of what you have just laid out for me . . .

MINISTER: Well that would be very nice for your countrymen, but much too risky for you . . .

DIANA: *(Vehemently.)* I must witness what you've just told me. I want to get to the very heart of this matter!

MINISTER: I don't think you have any idea what you'd be getting into . . . I'm sorry but I can't, I won't support this initiative of yours.

DIANA: Please help me — I'm going to do it anyway, it's crucial for me — my father was killed by the drug mafia. Don't worry, I'm not looking for revenge. If my life has any meaning at all, it's through confronting this problem, which has so affected me since I was a very little girl . . . It may be possible to do something even now . . . and you're very concerned about this too . . . Why don't we work out a plan together?

MINISTER: Why don't you go to the CIA? They have the same information, but researched, revised, and up to date . . . also, they can give you something I can't. Protection.

DIANA: If you don't want to get involved, I understand. As for the CIA, I would hope they don't find out what I am up to.

(The minister looks at her fixedly.)

MINISTER: You're not a newspaper reporter, are you? I don't really understand who you are, but I believe in your reasons for proposing this . . . I'll tell you what. I'll give you the information you've asked for, the contacts and even a bit of protection. You see, I agree with you in avoiding the CIA — one never knows what their real interests are . . .

DIANA: When can we begin?

MINISTER: At your convenience . . .

HELEN: THANK YOU! Let's start this afternoon. With your help I can get in contact with the local drug traffickers.

(Flashy music. As Helen speaks, she changes clothes and puts on a provocative red dress; removes her wig, revealing a full head of curly black hair; applies colorful make-up and adopts a very sexy attitude. She goes to Cumbancha — the most popular salsa club in Medellin!)

HELEN: I didn't throw myself at the top bosses, I chose the under bosses. They're much easier to approach and have access to almost the same information as their bosses.

(Entering the club, Rosa de Guadalajara causes a sensation among the local ladies' men who gather around her. Rosa flirts with all of them but her attention is focused on Ramon, "The Cuban," who finally looks at her with undisguised lust. He orders his men to "bring her to my table." Rosa pays them no attention, acting indifferent. Finally Ramon realizes that if he wants to dance with her, he's going to have to ask her himself. Pouting, the Cuban leaves his table and comes over to Rosa. He grabs her by the arm and without exchanging a word, they begin to dance.)

(While Rosa embraces this sweaty awkward mole, hundreds of kilometers away, in Bogota, a group of men ambush Minister Lara Bonilla and riddle him with bullets.)

JACK: President Reagan's full responsibility for the Iran-Contra scandal will probably never be known, due to the destruction of certain documents by his employees. Lee Hamilton, President of the Bipartisan Commission of both houses addressed this point today . . .

HAMILTON: We close this historic trial, still not knowing if President Reagan was guilty or not of having ordered the Iran-Contras Operation, or of continuing, in a clandestine fashion, the war against Nicaragua in defiance of Congress. However, it is clear that the Chief of the White House did not exercise his Constitutional responsibility, making sure that the laws of the land were kept, and he did create the appropriate climate for the secret abuse of power, betrayal and disdain for the law.

ROSA DE GUADALAJARA: Ramon, "el Cubano's," work consisted of buying properties, arms and even complete factories to launder drug money. This made us travel constantly . . . especially to Panama.

(In a hotel in Panama, Rosa Guadalajara is being seduced by Ramon "el Cubano." Suddenly she gets up from the bed.)

ROSA: No. We're not making love today! I'm fed up. I have to stay shut up in hotels while you're out and about — I don't know where!

RAMON: I'm working, woman! That's why I'm here. To work!

ROSA: I don't believe you.

RAMON: Baby — that's your problem.

ROSA: Why don't you take me with you?

RAMON: What for?

ROSA: To make sure you really are working.

RAMON: You just got to take my word for it.

ROSA: Yeah? One night you'll come back and I won't be here.

(Ramon takes her face in his hands and squeezes it as if it were a rag.)

RAMON: You, you're here, quiet, until I get tired of you, you got it? Cuz if one night I get here and I don't find you — cuz you fell for somebody else, or for whatever, I'm gonna leave your face so that not even your sainted mother will recognize it.

(A kick in the balls ends the gorilla's diatribe. He writhes on the floor. The young woman takes his pistol and points it at him.)

ROSA: You, never touch me again, asshole! Because I'll kill you. I ain't one of your whores that you keep stashed away in bed in your hotel. No! If I'm with you, it's cuz I want to be with you, because I love you — but you either share your life with me and whatever it is you do, or I'm leaving — never mind your threats!

(She throws the gun at him and goes to the window. She's very emotional. There are tears in her eyes. Ramon looks at her surprised. He loosens up.)

RAMON: But what's your problem? Be patient, we're in the middle of a difficult operation — if it works out, we're gonna travel around the whole world.

ROSA: Ever since I've known you, you've been promising me things.

RAMON: I'm serious this time, you'll have jewels, your house . . .

ROSA: It's you I want.

RAMON: *(Proud.)* And you'll have me. I won't do nothing else except be with you the whole rest of the year. We'll travel in a beautiful yacht that I'm going to buy you . . .

ROSA: Go on, you're full of it — what kind of business can you do to earn enough to buy a yacht?

RAMON: This one.

ROSA: Yeah sure.

RAMON: Damn straight. This is the most important operation of my life.

ROSA: What's it got to do with?

RAMON: I ain't quite sure.

ROSA: What'd I tell you. The most important deal of your life and you won't even share it with me. Get away from me. I don't want to see you any-more.

RAMON: Listen, sweetheart, what I told you before is the truth. Even I'm not quite sure what's going down . . . it's like some kind of exchange with the gringos. A lot of cash is involved.

ROSA: *(Sitting on his lap.)* All right. You're almost convincing me.
(In Welles' office, the thunder of a helicopter landing distracts him from his reading. Welles goes to the window. O'Hara enters, very excited.)

O'HARA: There's a helicopter outside.

WELLES: I know. I'm not deaf. It's the Intelligence agents. Go get them and bring them on in.
(O'Hara exits embarrassed. Welles continues reading.)

ROSA: My relationship with Ramon, the Cuban, allowed me to discover an unusual secret operation between an American group and the Medellin Cartel: It seems, the Cartel would send arms, and transport equipment and dollars to the Nicaraguan Contras while the Americans would then facilitate an important drug shipment to the U.S. on the 24th of De-cember, taking advantage of the Christmas season.
(Ramon is putting on his clothes.)

ROSA: I still didn't know where in the United States they would unload the drugs and who would be behind such an agreement. *(To Ramon.)* So . . . you're leaving already?

RAMON: Yeah. I got a meeting at noon.

ROSA: *(Unconsolable.)* With those Americans?

RAMON: Yeah. They'll be here in Panama today.

ROSA: Are there some American women involved? *(Ramon smiles and shakes his head.)* Right . . . you're gonna tell me it's just business men or politi-cians.

RAMON: I ain't tellin you nothin more — for your own good. But they are real important people. They must be — imagine — to let us land a plane-load of drugs. But they're only here a coupla days, and then we're free to do what we please.
(He hurries to put on a large white sports coat and a straw hat.)

ROSA: I understood that I wouldn't be able to get the rest of the information — dates, names and other essential details from that animal and time was running out . . . *(To Ramon.)* So, what time do you think you'll be back?

RAMON: This afternoon. You can eat in the hotel.

ROSA: Don't be late. Cuz I'll be here waiting . . . to eat of course!

(They kiss. Ramon exits. The young woman dresses in a hurry.)

ROSA: Things were getting freakier all the time. I decided to follow him and get the rest of the information on my own . . . of course I was well aware that I was risking everything, but . . .

(The American embassy in Panama. Ramon arrives at the entrance. He shows his identification to the guards and they let him in. Rosa of Guadalajara arrives minutes later, wearing her best smile. But they won't let her enter. Understanding the futility of insisting, the young woman leaves. As she is leaving, she crosses paths with a military attaché. For a moment they look at each other curiously and then continue in opposite directions: Rosa to change her identity and the military attaché to Welles' office where he knocks on the door. Welles goes to open it.)

WELLES: Oh it's you. Come in. Come in.

(The military attaché enters and sits down on the big chair. Welles stays standing next to his desk. The men look each other over for a moment waiting for the other to speak. Welles begins.)

WELLES: We've kept the detained men isolated from each other and from the outside as you instructed.

MILITARY ATTACHÉ: Thank you, Commissioner.

WELLES: However, I'm not comfortable with all this. It's a little irregular . . .

MILITARY ATTACHÉ: It's absolutely normal when it comes to drug cases.

WELLES: There's no proof of drug connections with any of these men. I'm afraid this situation is going to come back at me. One of the detainees is a high official in the Mexican government. There'll be an official complaint lodged and quite an uproar.

MILITARY ATTACHÉ: We'll take care of the official complaint . . . and the uproar. Don't worry.

WELLES: I hope so. I'm about to retire and I don't want this to be a black mark on my record.

MILITARY ATTACHÉ: Your record won't be affected.

WELLES: Good. So . . . what are your instructions?

MILITARY ATTACHÉ: Hand the men over to us. From now on, we'll take charge of them.

WELLES: You're not going to take them to Chicago are you?

MILITARY ATTACHÉ: We have strict orders. Why? You got a problem?

WELLES: No, not at all . . . it's just that they were already interrogated. We've kept records of all of it, and I did offer them their freedom when you guys arrived. Really there are no charges against them. Also one of them is the father of the young man who killed himself. I'd like to see him released soon.

MILITARY ATTACHÉ: There are certain circumstances we have to clear up — the questioning's a little more extensive than usual.

WELLES: Well. *(He turns on the intercom.)* O'Hara, The men are being taken to Chicago . . . What? . . . yes, I understand . . . tell them that that's where they'll be set free.

(He checks visually with the attaché who nods his head.)

MILITARY ATTACHÉ: Are you going to go with them?

WELLES: Is it necessary?

MILITARY ATTACHÉ: Well, it'd be convenient . . . we want to make the transfer as official as possible.

WELLES: Okay.

MILITARY ATTACHÉ: Good. Thanks very much for your help, Commissioner.

WELLES: That's what I'm here for, Lieutenant?

MILITARY ATTACHÉ: Colonel.

WELLES: One more thing, before you go, Colonel.

MILITARY ATTACHÉ: Yes?

WELLES: In regards to the press — they've been calling. What will our official version of the crime be?

MILITARY ATTACHÉ: What kind of question is that, Commissioner? Do you think there's more than one version?

WELLES: I think there's no version at present.

MILITARY ATTACHÉ: A crime of passion — that's what it is. An older women gets involved with a younger man — who's also a drug dealer. He goes crazy with drugs and kills her. Later, realizing what he's done, he kills himself . . . you don't believe that's what happened?

WELLES: I think there's some discrepancies.

MILITARY ATTACHÉ: What do you mean?

WELLES: The boy's father doesn't think it was a suicide. He thinks his son was murdered.

MILITARY ATTACHÉ: What made him think that?

WELLES: His son is left-handed so it doesn't seem logical or easy that he shot himself in the heart.

MILITARY ATTACHÉ: *(Thinking for a moment.)* Well, no that isn't logical. This

affair of theirs becomes even more tangled when we add that the woman who was killed was a DEA officer . . . *(He studies Welles.)*
Were you aware of that?

WELLES: *(Surprised.)* No!

MILITARY ATTACHÉ: Doesn't it seem strange?

WELLES: Very!

MILITARY ATTACHÉ: That's what makes this case even more sensitive — and why these men are still being held. You see, even though the woman had taken a leave of absence from the DEA, it seems she was doing some investigations of her own.

WELLES: I see.

MILITARY ATTACHÉ: However — in spite of that — a crime of passion still seems like the only logical choice . . . can you think of another one?

WELLES: *(Undecided.)* Me? No. Not right away.

MILITARY ATTACHÉ: Me neither; and if it isn't exactly logical that he used his right hand to shoot himself, it can be explained by the wound on his other hand and the lack of space in the car . . . or simply an attempt to create false speculations . . . don't you think?

WELLES: Well . . . sure, that could be the reason.

MILITARY ATTACHÉ: I think . . . yes. We should officially close the case. It would get rid of a whole tangle of speculation, especially by the press — and that would allow us to continue our investigation with less scrutiny and without the pressure of public opinion.

WELLES: I'm not sure I agree. If we take the men being held, they're going to demand a very public investigation.

MILITARY ATTACHÉ: We'll try to talk them out of it. It shouldn't be hard. If the investigation remains open, as suspects, they will be most affected.
(He gets up and approaches the commissioner.)

MILITARY ATTACHÉ: But actually, it's your opinion I'm interested in, Commissioner. Would you agree that further investigation should be carried out in this manner?

WELLES: We'll do whatever you ask us, sir.
(In Panama, the journalist Diana Rand arrives at the American embassy, identifies herself to the guards and is allowed to pass.)

DIANA: It wasn't easy to find the location of the meeting. I decided to stand and wait in a general access hallway to see what I could see.
(A group of people, Ramon among them, guided by a military attaché. The same one who crossed paths with her before and who was with Welles in the

preceding scene — appears in the hallway. The men are talking softly among themselves. Diana follows them at a discreet distance.)

DIANA: It wasn't the best time to find out who they were or get any information; however, I could see one of them — a military man who carried a package under his arm. I make out the words Drugs For Medical Use, and a destination, Mexico, USA!

(This image is reinforced by a photograph on the screen.)

DIANA: I could see they were heading towards some trucks with a series of storage areas behind them. I waited until they left. Then I made my way over to make sure of what I'd seen — that these trucks — with Ramon's business logo — were loaded with arms, and that the storage rooms were stocked with hundreds of packages like the one the military attaché was carrying!

(She changes her wig and clothes and becomes Helen Esparza.)

HELEN: Believe me, I didn't stick around with that kind of information. I was burning to tell someone. So I changed my identity again — this time to my own and took the first plane back to Chicago . . .

(While a plane crosses the air — lights up on a room where a group of young people are working at computers.)

HELEN: From the airport I went directly to my office.

(Offices of the DEA in Chicago. Through a window we see her entering the office and being greeted with hugs and affection by her coworkers. The young woman takes some documents from her purse and hands them over. The young people start to analyze them on their computers.)

HELEN: The entire office was astonished by the results of this bit of undercover work and wanted to analyze it immediately.

(Louis, a young man, approaches Helen with a broad grin. The others exchange knowing looks and return to their work. Helen turns and, when she sees him, her face brightens.)

HELEN: Louis!

(Louis embraces her and then leads her into his office where they kiss passionately.)

LOUIS: You don't know what you've put me through, you! Months without even a word! Jesus!

HELEN: I can't believe how much I've missed you!

(They kiss again. Tim, a fat freckled young man, enters.)

TIM: Okay. This is the deal. On December 20th, they leave Barranquilla for Panama on Southern Airlines. And listen to this! That same plane leaves

Panama on the 22nd, picks up some horses from a Mexican equestrian team and takes them to St. Louis, Missouri on December 25th!

HELEN: So it's one day later than I thought.

TIM: No my dear Watson, the drugs will be delivered the day before!

HELEN: But how will they get through Mexican customs?

TIM: Let's see . . . a certain Carlos Gonzalez, an official of the Mexican government, will be receiving the horses in Saint Louis.

HELEN: No, no, no . . . Mexico — USA was clearly written on the packages — there's got to be a connection between the two countries.

COLLIE: I think you've got it wrong. The drugs were addressed to a place in the USA called Mexico.

TIM: Yeah — otherwise the USA would be the addressee and the sender would be Mexico.

HELEN: You mean there is a place called Mexico in the U.S.?

BECKY: Actually there's four. One in Indiana, another in Maine, in Missouri and in the state of New York — which one do you prefer?

HELEN: The one that has an airport.

BECKY: None of them do. They're all real small towns. The one in Indiana has a population of 860, New York 1621, Maine 3325, and let's see . . . wait . . . the one in Missouri isn't that small, thirteen thousand people live there!

TIM: Yeah. And get this — it's surrounded by prairie, famous for its race horses, and its clay-based soil could very easily camouflage a hidden airport!

BECKY: It's real close to St. Louis, where the horses are going.

COLLIE: They could unload there without having to change their route.

HELEN: You guys are great!

TIM: Yeah? Just don't forget us when you get a promotion!
    (They laugh. They get their coats and start to leave. Becky comes back.)

BECKY: We are so happy you're back!
    (The others laugh and imitate her. Helen blows them a kiss and finally remains alone with Louis.)

HELEN: Finally! It seems like a dream . . . being here . . . knowing that I'll be in my own house tonight, having dinner with you — you better be coming over! (Louis smiles.) . . . and that great feeling you get when it seems like all the work you've put in is going to mean something!

LOUIS: What're you going to do next?

HELEN: I'll go to Mexico, Missouri, and find the local contacts. Ramon mentioned one. They call him "El Mexicano," but he's not Mexican. I've got to make sure they haven't changed the original plan or switched the dates.

Then we've got to get everything ready to dismantle the operation and arrest everyone involved.

LOUIS: Okay — I'll arrange a meeting with the CIA.

HELEN: No!

LOUIS: Talk to them. We'll get their help!

HELEN: Their help? Why?

LOUIS: We don't know where they're going to unload. If we want to control the drop-off — we'd have to cover the whole county. Do you know what that would involve? A lot more manpower than our organization can provide.

HELEN: If I can pinpoint the drop-off spot, it won't be so complicated. Let me try that first. We've still got a few weeks to go.

LOUIS: Okay my love, whatever you say . . .

HELEN: But . . . I could use some help in finding a decent job, some ID and a commission to go to Mexico, Missouri.

LOUIS: Give me a couple of days.

HELEN: As far as my new identity . . . *(She shakes out her hair and piles it coquettishly on top of her head.) . . .* What do you think of "Ruth Gordon"? *(Once again we hear the deafening roar of a helicopter and O'Hara erupts again into Welles' office. Welles jumps, startled . . .)*

WELLES: Damn it, O'Hara. Knock, will you?

O'HARA: I'm sorry, sir. All the prisoners are on the helicopter. They're waiting for you!

(Welles is reluctant to leave. He hasn't finished reading the letter.)

WELLES: Look, you go instead. I've got a lot to do. It's only a matter of handing them over. But, make sure we have some documentation that we delivered and the men were received.

O'HARA: Whatever you like, sir.

(He is about to exit, but stops for a moment.)

WELLES: What?

O'HARA: I didn't bring my raincoat and it's pouring out.

WELLES: Okay, Okay . . . you can take mine and my hat. I'll probably still be here when you get back anyway.

O'HARA: Thanks.

(He puts on the hat and coat and exits happily.)

RUTH: However, something happened the day before I left — which I'm a little unsure how to account for. Louis urgently called me into his office. *(The office. Louis is very nervous. Helen enters smiling.)*

HELEN: Yes? You wanted to talk?

LOUIS: *(Doesn't know how to begin.)* Helen, don't take this the wrong way . . . but . . . they've assigned Nolan to take charge of the operation.

HELEN: What operation?

LOUIS: Mexico, USA!

HELEN: Nolan? . . . I don't understand. What does Nolan know about this operation?

LOUIS: What you're going to tell him. They thought this would be an especially high risk mission for you . . . and frankly, I agree with them . . .

HELEN: Who are "them"?

LOUIS: The Agency.

HELEN: You told them everything?

LOUIS: I couldn't very well hide what I was doing . . . but they're happy, very pleased, they're even considering you for a promotion and public recognition once this case is concluded.

HELEN: But Nolan's an idiot. You know that! If they give him this job . . . no way! It'll ruin everything.

LOUIS: He'll be well supervised. You can keep tabs on him yourself!

HELEN: You're starting to sound condescending.

LOUIS: I'm concerned for your safety, all right?

HELEN: Forget about my safety! Louis, forget that shit — Don't talk to me like an official. Talk to me like the man I love, the man who understands me . . . What's really going on?

(Louis is alarmed and makes signs that she shouldn't continue speaking. He gets his coat and invites her to go out with him so they can talk more freely. As they leave, he says, as if into a microphone . . .)

LOUIS: Don't be silly. There's nothing going on. Don't get paranoid on me. Look, it's only that we have a responsibility to look out for your safety. You're very valuable to us, all of us. Come on — I'll walk you to your car.

(They leave the office and begin to walk.)

LOUIS: The truth is, I don't understand shit. At first they were so enthusiastic. Then, all of a sudden, it changed. Now they say a drug operation like that would be impossible in this country and that you're either obsessed with a personal vendetta or you'll go after a promotion any way you can . . .

HELEN: You know that's not true!

LOUIS: Of course. But they're the ones making the decisions; they don't want your investigation to go any further. They're only sending Nolan, obviously, to keep up appearances.

HELEN: But, Louis . . . will you keep helping me?

LOUIS: To do what?

HELEN: You know me. I can't stop now.

LOUIS: Uh-uh. No Helen! No way. It won't work. You've touched a soft spot somehow — we don't know what's going on underneath or who might be implicated in this operation.

HELEN: I don't care. I didn't enter the agency to protect "whoever might be implicated in this operation" — no matter how high a position they may have!

LOUIS: You don't get it!

HELEN: So explain.

LOUIS: Sometimes the government is involved in complicated negotiations that on the surface seem pretty shady but that have to do with our national security, our image abroad or some kind of prickly political machinations that we're in no position to judge. We're on the inside. We're limited. Our best weapon's discretion, and above all, loyalty!

HELEN: Loyalty to whom?

LOUIS: To our institutions!

HELEN: What about our loyalty to human beings?! I might not know what political maneuvers are behind all this or if my work affects "our image abroad," but there is something I do know, something concrete — and that is that someone — at a very high level and for whatever reasons, is giving his permission to poison our people, our children — and I'm going to try to stop it in any way I can. If you're with me, help me; if not, do whatever you think is right. *(She exits.)*

(The ringing of the phone distracts Welles.)

WELLES: Commissioner Welles speaking. Yes. . . what? . . . when? Of course, I'll be there immediately!

(He looks for his overcoat and doesn't find it. He exits swearing a blue streak.)

JACK: In an opinion poll conducted by *The Washington Post* and ABC it was revealed that sixty-three percent of the population think that the President should give a presidential pardon to his associates, at least to North and Poindexter, to prevent them from being unjustly persecuted by the law. For his part, Colonel North, or "Ollie-Rambo" as the young people call him, has a bright future. He was offered over two million dollars for his biography and a half million dollars for the television rights to his adventures in international politics.

(A photo appears on screen with the words: Military helicopter crashes.)

JACK: A United States Army helicopter UH-1 brushed an electric wire and crashed near Chicago today. All occupants were killed, including four civilians; police commissioner for Mexico County, Missouri, Norman Welles, and two soldiers from the National Guard. Apparently the helicopter was part of an anti-drug mission.

(At the site of the disaster, a surprised female journalist finds Commissioner Welles looking at the burned rubble.)

REPORTER: Commissioner Welles! What a surprise! You were reported as one of the victims.

WELLES: Yeah. Well I should have been on that flight.

REPORTER: Could you tell us something about the accident? Who were the victims?

WELLES: The policeman who died was Don O'Hara. He worked with me. The other four were civilians detained in the Ruth Gordon case.

REPORTER: Why were they aboard an army helicopter?

WELLES: Bad luck . . .

(He turns away and leaves.)

REPORTER: *(Flustered.)* We'll continue with more news . . . Jack . . .

JACK: The latest opinion polls show that President Reagan's reputation has not been harmed at all by the Iran-Contra affair or his defiance of Congress or for inciting the murder of several Nicaraguan citizens. He continues to be the most popular president here in decades and his influence will be a decisive element in the next election if Vice President George Bush is to become president.

(Commissioner Welles enters his office, goes to his desk and again takes out the letter and starts reading.)

RUTH: As soon as I got settled in Mexico, Missouri, I began to hunt for "El Mexicano." It wasn't easy; his nickname gave me several false leads because I started to look for him among the Mexican population *(On the screen appear the faces of Nick, Al, Carlos, Tiro and Alvy.)* However, one of them, an ex-drug addict called Alvy, did put me in contact with "el Mexicano" — who, by the way, wasn't Mexican, but Colombian.

(Nick's cafe. Ruth Gordon with El Mexicano.)

RUTH: This jewel, besides being a mercenary and an ex-CIA agent, was one of the contacts for Operation Mexico, Missouri. *(To El Mexicano.)* You know what I want for Christmas? I want you to take me to Las Vegas!

EL MEXICANO: I can't go for Christmas. We'll go later.

RUTH: Oh! Well then — what are we going to do for Christmas?

EL MEXICANO: You are going to disappear.

RUTH: You're leaving me?

EL MEXICANO: For just a few days. Why don't you have Christmas with your family anyway? . . .

RUTH: This confirmed the date of shipment — so I didn't need this jerk for anything anymore . . . *(She gets up from the table.)* Fine. I'm going to the ladies room.

(She gets her things, leaves the cafe, gets in her car and starts it up.)

EL MEXICANO: Hey, wait listen, Ruth!

RUTH: Now I only had to find the airport where the shipment was going to be taken. Alvy also helped me with this. He found us a small crop duster that belonged to a friend . . . what a lovely young man. He never knew about my double life. He thought I only wanted to take some photos of the town for my magazine. He was bubbling over with enthusiasm . . .

(In a small crop dusting plane the young people fly over the county. Ruth takes pictures as they talk in shouts.)

RUTH: Okay. I'm done with the town. Let's go out into the countryside!

ALVY: Which do you want — open fields or mountains!?!

RUTH: Open fields and mountains!

(They laugh and joke around. Ruth is taking photos of everything.)

RUTH: What's that?

ALVY: Where?

RUTH: Between those two hills . . . it looks like an airstrip.

ALVY: I don't know. I never saw it before.

RUTH: Let's go take a look.

ALVY: Yeah, but that's outside the county!

RUTH: I don't care . . . could you fly between these hills?

ALVY: Absolutely. If you asked me to I'd fly under them. Only look, there's a little shack and some soldiers signaling us!

RUTH: Don't stop . . . we better keep going!

ALVY: I think it's some military installation . . . look at all the signs that say no trespassing. Shit!

RUTH: That road to the right — is that an airstrip?

ALVY: Yeah, it could be.

RUTH: Fly over it for me.

ALVY: I'll try.

(Some explosions warn them that they are trespassing.)

ALVY: Hey — I think they're firing at us.

RUTH: Yeah — let's get out of here

(We hear more shots.)

ALVY: I can't turn the plane. It's too sharp a turn. Okay — grab on — I'll have to fly across as fast as I can . . . *(The plane accelerates and leaves the military base followed by a concert of explosions.)*

RUTH: The photos confirmed my assessment: The military base had an airstrip, and most likely that's where the drugs would be unloaded. This made my experiences in Colombia and Panama and the agency's final decision much clearer, but it changed my strategy concerning the landing. *(She goes to a telephone and dials.)* I always tried to avoid third-party involvement in my work, but this time I desperately needed help . . . Hello, Alvy?

(In the kitchen, Janet hears the phone ring and tactlessly tries to get closer. She listens to part of the conversation.)

RUTH: No Alvy — what I need is for someone from the military base to tell me about its inner workings . . . he had to have a drug contact in the army itself . . . No, I can't tell you any more — but it's really important to me. Yes? Good. I'll wait for your call. *(She hangs up.)* I needed inside information about the base. Otherwise it was going to be very difficult to keep the plane from landing without calling in the CIA — which I wanted to avoid at all costs

(The telephone rings. Ruth hurries to answer it.)

RUTH: Hello. Alvy? Yes? . . . *(Happy.)* Great! Where? Tell him we can meet at Nick's at eight. You don't know how much I want to thank you. *(She hangs up and then picks up the receiver again.)* I forgot to ask him the military person's name. I picked up the phone to see if he was still on the line, and I heard a discrete "click," which made me suspect that the telephone was tapped. I checked it out immediately.

(She takes out a small gadget which she connects to the telephone. She dials a number. A little light goes on when someone answers.)

RUTH: I'm looking for Joe Flores. He's not there? Sorry. *(She hangs up rapidly. The lights takes a few seconds longer to go out.)*

RUTH: The line was tapped! And in a student apartment! This meant the agency was well aware of my activities in town — and maybe the drug traffickers as well. My first impulse was to get the hell out of the county and take my information to the press — but that would alert the drug mafia and they could simply postpone the operation. That's when I wrote these letters and went to St. Louis.

(The young woman puts on her coat and leaves. On screen we see the following headline: Case Against Oliver North fails.)

JACK: By preventing the disclosure of certain documents, for reasons of national security, President Reagan has caused the case brought against Oliver North for his activities in the Iran-Contra scandal to be dismissed. The two principal charges were withdrawn this week by Prosecutor Lawrence

Walsh. It's thought that the same criteria will be applied to others involved in this case.

(At the Greyhound station, Ruth puts the letters in the locker. She then goes to a phone booth.)

RUTH: Louis? Paloma Blanca here, advising you that I made a date with someone in the military, who is apparently prepared to hand over some key information about the landing. But it could be a trap — so I'm asking for your protection. The date is for tonight — you know the town — at a cafe called Nick's.

JACK: In Colombia the drug Czar Jorge Ochoa was freed from La Picota prison today after being held for five weeks. Two days before, District Attorney, Mauro Hoyos was shot and killed at the Medellin airport. Unable to control the violence, Colombian authorities seem to have given up against the drug lords and have begun to officially consider that the drug trade be made legal in their country . . .

(In her apartment Ruth has put on the dress she wore in the first scene. Janet enters and is surprised to see her getting dressed up.)

RUTH: Janet, I'm going out.

JANET: I thought we were having dinner!

RUTH: I might be back in time, but I can't promise.

JANET: But you asked me only yesterday!

RUTH: Something important's come up all of a sudden. Anyway, listen, I'll really try to be back in time. I promise.

JANET: I made a shrimp curry . . . the kind you like so much

RUTH: I'll try. I promise Janet . . . I want to ask you a favor, a big one.

JANET: Of course.

RUTH: This key goes to a locker at the Greyhound Bus Terminal in St. Louis. There's some letters there — they're already addressed and stamped. Promise me . . . promise me that if anything were to happen to me, whatever it might be, that you'll mail those letters . . . no. Don't say a word. Just promise me!

JANET: *(Frightened.)* I promise you . . . but!

RUTH: Shhhhh. Swear to me that no matter what happens you will never tell anyone about this. No one. Swear it!

JANET: Okay . . .

RUTH: Now, just be calm because nothing is going to happen. But in case of emergency, I did want to leave knowing that I can trust you . . .

JANET: You can trust me absolutely . . . more than anyone!

RUTH: I know and thank you for being such a lovely person.

(She gives Janet a kiss and leaves. Janet begins to cry.)

(A cold wind shakes the windows of Commissioner Welles' office and he goes to make sure they're closed. Ruth takes the same position she had at the beginning of the letter. Welles sits down to read more.)

RUTH: My only hope now is that my letters will be published in the newspapers so that this investigation, which has cost me so dearly, will be made public and will be judged by the American people . . . maybe then my sacrifice won't have been in vain . . .

(Welles shudders and closes the letter. All of a sudden Bill, the young policeman, is almost at his elbow.)

WELLES: Bill! How did you get in here?

BILL: Your door was open, Commissioner.

WELLES: I didn't think anyone would be around this late!

BILL: I stayed behind to see if you needed anything.

WELLES: Thanks, but I'm fine, you can go.

BILL: You sure?

WELLES: I'm very sure.

BILL: Okay — well, have a good evening, Commissioner . . .

(He exits but you can see his silhouette as he stands to one side of the door. Bill draws a pistol. The commissioner sees this reflected in the window. He takes out his own pistol and is ready to defend himself. He thinks again. He considers the futility of what he is about to do and goes back to his desk. He takes out the letters and looks at them. Finally he puts them in an ashtray and sets them on fire.)

(Bill leaves. The flames grow until they engulf Ruth Gordon.)

RUTH: No! . . . Nooooo! . . . Nooooo!

(Black Out.)

END OF PLAY

OCOTEPEC, 1989